THE
OLYMPICS
FOR BEGINNERS®

THE

OLYMPICS
FOR BEGINNERS®

BRANDON TOROPOV
ILLUSTRATED BY: JOE LEE
RESEARCHER: STEPHEN TOROPOV

FOR BEGINNERS® • 2008

For Beginners LLC
62 East Starrs Plain Road
Danbury, CT 06810 USA
www.forbeginnersbooks.com

Text: © 2008 Brandon Yusuf Toropov
Illustrations: © 2008 Joe Lee
Cover Art © 2008 Joe Lee
Cover Design: David Janik, DavidJanik.net
Book Design: iWordSmith.com

A For Beginners® Documentary Comic Book
Copyright © 2008

Cataloging-in-Publication information is available from the Library of Congress.

ISBN-10 # 1-934389-33-1 Trade
ISBN-13 # 978-1-934389-33-1 Trade

Manufactured in the United States of America

For Beginners® and Beginners Documentary Comic Books® are published
by For Beginners LLC.

First Edition

Contact Brandon Yusuf Toropov at: btoropov@iWordSmith.com

SINCERE THANKS TO: DAWN RESHEN-DOTY, MERRILEE WARHOLAK, JULIA TOROPOV, JUDITH BURROS, AND THERESA NWAIRAT FOR THEIR SUPPORT AND ASSISTANCE ON THIS PROJECT. WITHOUT STEPHEN TOROPOV'S DILIGENT RESEARCH, THIS BOOK WOULD NOT EXIST.

IN MEMORY OF YURI TOROPOV.

CONTENTS

Answers to rear cover quiz

THE QUESTION WAS ... *CAN YOU NAME THE OLYMPIC HEROES WHO WENT ON TO CAREERS IN SHOW BUSINESS?* AND THE ANSWERS ARE (STARTING FROM UPPER LEFT-HAND CORNER):

SWIMMER *JOHNNY WEISSMULLER* (1924 AND 1928 MEDALIST) AS TARZAN.

FIGURE SKATER *SONJA HENIE* (1928, 1932, AND 1936 MEDALIST) AS, WELL, SONJA HENIE.

WEIGHTLIFTER *HAROLD SAKATA* (1948 MEDALIST) AS THE VILLAIN "ODDJOB" IN THE JAMES BOND THRILLER *GOLDFINGER.*

GYMNAST *CATHY RIGBY* (MEMBER OF 1968 AND 1972 U.S. OLYMPIC TEAMS) AS PETER PAN.

SWIMMER *BUSTER CRABBE* (1932 MEDALIST) AS FLASH GORDON.

2

Introduction

WHY CAN'T WE BE FRIENDS?

Could national rivalries play out on the field of athletic competition, rather than the field of battle? The Olympic Games, both old and new, have always been about that question. That means that they have always, to at least some degree, been about politics, despite some eloquent protests to the contrary.

In this book, you'll learn about the noble ideals, the awesome spectacle, and, above all, the athletic excellence that has made the Olympics the primary global event of our time. At the same time, you'll learn about the times that those ideals were compromised, the times the spectacle was interrupted by tragedy, and the times the athletic excellence was compromised by a willingness to bend or break the rules.

You will learn, in these pages, about humanity itself, in conflict and at peace, at its best and at its worst, as it has reflected itself through the great prism of the Olympic Games. If that story is of interest ... and we think it is a remarkable story indeed ... read on.

Part One:
The Ancient Games

Nobody knows how it all started

HEY ... IT WAS ANCIENT WHEN I *GOT* HERE...

All we know for sure is *where* it started: Ancient Greece. At some point between 704 B.C. and 884 B.C., rival city-states were taking part in a series of athletic competitions that were held every fourth summer. During these games, military conflict took a back seat to sports.

The Games became steadily more important, reaching a high point in infuence and prestige around the sixth century B.C.

A number of myths arose to explain how the Games came about ...

Here's the big one...

SUPPOSEDLY, THE DEMIGOD *HERAKLES* (HERCULES) FOUNDED THE OLYMPICS TO HONOR HIS FATHER *ZEUS*. (*MT. OLYMPUS*, GREECE'S HIGHEST MOUNTAIN, WAS CONSIDERED THE HOME OF THE GODS.)

AFTER HE COMPLETED HIS FAMOUS TWELVE LABORS, HERAKLES BUILT THE *FIRST OLYMPIC STADIUM*.

ACCORDING TO LEGEND, IT WAS *CALLED* A "STADIUM" BECAUSE IT WAS 400 OF HERAKLES' STRIDES LONG. THAT UNIT OF DISTANCE BECAME KNOWN AS A "STADION." THIS IS 400 METERS IN MODERN TERMS, THE CIRCUMFERENCE OF THE MAIN SPORTING VENUE.

THAT OLD TIME RELIGION

THE ANCIENT OLYMPIC GAMES WERE STEEPED IN **PAGAN RITUAL,** AND FEATURED SACRIFICES TO THE GODS **ZEUS** AND **PELOPS.**

THE COMPETITION WAS ORIGINALLY LIMITED TO **FOOTRACES,** BUT EVENTUALLY GREW TO INCLUDE THE PENTATHLON (RUNNING, LONG JUMP, WRESTLING, SPEAR THROWING, AND DISCUS THROWING), BOXING, CHARIOT RACING, AND OTHER SPORTS.

VICTORIOUS ATHLETES WERE CROWNED WITH OLIVE LEAVES AND WON **SPECIAL STATUS.** THEY HAD TO TRAIN FOR MONTHS, AND SPENT 30 STRAIGHT DAYS UNDER THE WATCHFUL EYES OF ORGANIZERS. THERE WERE STRICT RULES ON WHO COULD AND COULDN'T COMPETE. (WOMEN AND SLAVES, FOR INSTANCE, WERE FORBIDDEN.)

USUALLY, ANCIENT OLYMPIC ATHLETES COMPETED **NAKED,** AN OPTION THAT MODERN OLYMPIC ORGANIZERS HAVE NOT YET EMBRACED.

THINK OF THE **RATINGS!**

The Games go down ...

WHAT HAVE THE ROMANS GOT AGAINST *TRUCES,* ANYWAY?

Despite a thousand-year history that included both athletic glory and occasional excuses to step away from armed conflict, the Olympics could not survive the Roman Empire.

The Games were discontinued in 393 A.D., by the Emperor Theodosius I, who disliked their pagan roots and considered them to conflict with the official religion of the Empire, Christianity.

... BECAUSE YOU CAN ONLY KEEP A **GREAT IDEA** DOWN FOR SO LONG!

10

Part Two:
The Amateur Ideal

The good doctor

EUREKA! WE'LL RESTAGE THE OLYMPICS ... RIGHT HERE IN SHROPSHIRE!

The modern idea of resurrecting the Olympic ideal can be traced to a nineteenth-century English doctor, **William Penny Brookes** (above).

Brookes organized a competition in 1850 "for the promotion of the moral, physical, and intellectual improvement of the inhabitants of the town and neighborhood of Wenlock and especially of the working classes." The contest was called the Olympian Class, and was eventually renamed the Wenlock Olympian Society Annual Games. Two interesting events followed.

In 1859, a Greek philanthropist sponsored the first revival of the ancient Olympic games in Athens.

And in 1890, a well-connected French bureaucrat named Pierre de Coubertin traveled to Shropshire and met with Brookes, who was still running the Wenlock contests as an annual event.

IF WE STICK TO OUR IDEALS, WE'LL HAVE LESS **WAR!** RIGHT?

De Coubertin, who was on a fact-finding mission to learn about sports in English public schools, had a vision. If the young people of the world would compete on a prominent international stage, they could promote global harmony and bring nations closer together. When he saw the games in Shrophsire, and spoke at length with Brookes, he concluded that an international Olympic movement, resurrecting the spirit of the ancient Greek Games, could turn his pacifist ideal into a reality.

De Coubertin's vision was heavily influenced by Brookes's work, and by the athletic contests he saw in the English public school system, which emphasized amateurism. He drew out his vision at a conference at the Sorbonne University in Paris in 1894. Not long after that ...

De Coubertin founded the International Olympic Committee, and scheduled its inaugural International Games for Athens in the year 1896.

The roll call

AS A CONCESSION TO THE GREEKS, I GOT TO BE THE FIRST PRESIDENT... BUT PIERRE TOOK OVER AFTER THE *ATHENS GAMES.*

DEMETRIUS VIKELAS

Presidents of the International Olympic Committee:

DEMETRIUS VIKELAS (1894-1896)

PIERRE DE COUBERTIN (1896-1925)

GODEFROY DE BLONAY (ACTING 1916-1919)

HENRI DE BAILLET-LATOUR (1925-1942)

SIGFRID EDSTRÖM (1942-1952)

AVERY BRUNDAGE (1952-1972)

LORD KILLANIN (1972-1980)

JUAN ANTONIO SAMARANCH (1980-2001)

JACQUES ROGGE (2001-CURRENT)

But we're getting ahead of ourselves.

The year is still 1896, and the very first episode of what would eventually become the most popular ongoing sports drama on earth is about to play out.

The opening scene of this extraordinary global spectacle is set in ...

Athens: Back to the Future

The 1896 Olympics, the first modern Games, were held in Athens, Greece, as a salute to the ancient legacy of the original Olympics. One highlight: Greek shepherd and water-seller **Spyridon Louis's** first-place finish in the marathon, a classical Greek athletic contest inspired by the story of an ancient messenger who supposedly ran twenty-six miles to announce an Athenian victory. Louis's win was rich in symbolism for the home-town crowd, which had been growing a bit restless. Earlier in the Games, American Bob Garrett had won the discus throw, a major disappointment for local fans hoping to reclaim past glory and honor a home-grown champion in a truly "Greek" event.

Louis thus became a focal point in the first modern re-staging of the Olympics. A national hero, he shunned the spotlight after his victory, choosing to resume work on his father's farm.

YEAH, YEAH ... THE OLD "WATER-SELLER CAN'T WIN A MARATHON" STEREOTYPE. WATCH THIS.

Low by today's standards, the total number of countries and athletes participating in Athens in 1896 (14 and 241, respectively) nevertheless represented the largest gathering of countries ever assembled for an international sporting event up to that time.

No women, please.

NOT THAT WE'RE *SEXIST* OR ANYTHING...

Opening ceremonies at the 1896 Olympics. No female athletes were in attendance. Baron de Coubertin regarded the possibility of women competing as "impractical, uninteresting, unaestehtic, and incorrect."

The Games Begin

80,000 PEOPLE SHOWED UP FOR THE BRIEF OPENING CEREMONY.

THE ROWING EVENT WAS CANCELED DUE TO *HIGH WINDS.*

A COUPLE OF PROBLEMS ALONG THE WAY ... BUT WE DID IT!

THE YACHTING EVENT WAS CANCELED DUE TO A *LACK OF YACHTS.*

Golden moments....

The first athletic event to crown a champion was the hop, step, and jump – a scheduling decision that made American James B. Connolly, of Massachusetts, the first modern Olympic champion. Connolly received a medal and a laurel wreath ...The medal for first-place finishers in Athens in 1896 was *silver*, not gold; second-place finishers got a bronze medal ...German Carl Schuhmann won three gymnastics titles – and also came in first place in Greco-Roman wrestling! ... Launceston Elliot of Great Britain and Viggo Jensen of Denmark came in tied at the end of a two-handed weightlifting event. The judges ruled that Jensen had displayed better stylein his lifts and declared him the winner, a decision that led to a protest from Great Britain but was not overturned. (Elliot came in first in the single-handed event, which immediately followed.)

1900: The Uncertain Olympics

Ambiguity reigns in Paris. The formal status of the 1900 Games was deeply uncertain. The contests were combined with (and dwarfed by) the World's Fair in Paris of that year. Despite an impressive promotional effort and some cool posters, a fair number of the participants appear never to have fully grasped that what they were competing in had anything to do with Athens in 1896.

There were no opening or closing ceremonies, and the prizes handed out featured no direct reference to the Olympic movement. Retroactively, the winners were regarded as honest-to-goodness Olympic champions.

Call them the "P.R. Games." They built greater visibility into the Olympic movement, but lacked the focus of the 1896 Athens gathering, what with that shiny new Eiffel Tower stealing all the focus.

SPORTING EVENTS USUALLY SKIPPED THE WORD "OLYMPIC"!

Coming off the success of 1896, the Greeks had argued that the Games should be permanently based in their country, since Greece was the historical birthplace of the ancient Olympic contests. The IOC had other ideas. The world was assembling in Paris for the World's Fair, and de Coubertin wanted the Games to be part of it. In order to be included in the Fair, however, the IOC ended up having to release control of the Games to a subcommittee created by Fair organizers, who treated the events as a sideshow. The stage for the 1900 Games was indeed global, as de Coubertin had wished ... but he found, before long, that he had been upstaged.

Thanks for the vote of support.

"A *USELESS* AND *ABSURD* ACTIVITY."

Alfred Picard, the director of the 1900 World's Fair, on atheletic competition.

Paris Plays ... Uniquely

These competitions debuted at the 1900 Paris Olympics, never to be staged again:

LIVE *PIGEON* SHOOTING.

ARE YOU KIDDING ME?

SWIMMING THROUGH AN *OBSTACLE* COURSE.

WHAT'S NEXT? ALLIGATORS?

THE TWO-DAY *CRICKET* MATCH.

NEXT TIME -- A MONTH-LONG CONTEST!

Golden moments....

Three roommates from the University of Pennsylvania (Alvin Kraenzlein, Irving Baxter, and John Tewskbury) combined with Purdue alumnus Ray Ewrry to lead the American assualt on the track and field events. The quartet combined for eleven victories, five second-place finishes, and a third-place finish ... The fencing competition was open to professionals; Frenchman Albert Robert Ayat not only came in first, but received (gasp!) 3000 francs to honor his achievement .... For the first time, women were allowed to compete in Olympic sporting events, but this concession to the egalitarian impulse is limited. Only golf and tennis were open to the ladies. Britain's Charlotte Cooper became the first female Olympic champion with her victory in the ladies' singles, then went on to help secure a first-place finish in the mixed doubles event.

1904: Meet Me in St. Louis

FINISH LINE ... AND MAKE IT *SNAPPY!*

Creativity, if not integrity, marks the most infamous controversy of the 1904 St. Louis games. Crowds cheered U.S. marathoner **Fred Lorz,** the first competitor to make his way into the stadium and cross the finish line. Eager photographers snapped his picture as he posed with the daughter of the President of the United States.

Officials were preparing to award Lorz the gold medal when someone figured out that he had run nine miles, hopped a ride in a car for the next *eleven* miles, and finished the last six on foot. Lorz was booted off the victory stand, and the medal was awarded to the man everyone initially thought had finished second, Thomas Hicks. Lorz was disgraced ... but he wasn't the only "whatever it takes" athlete that day. Hicks had received a strychnine injection to boost his stamina. Nobody made a big deal about that at the time, though.

George Eyser, a U.S. gymnast, secured two first-place finishes, one second-place finish, and a third-place finish. Quite a performance ... especially when you consider that Eyser had a wooden leg.

NO. REALLY. I CAME IN *FIRST.* LET ME SHOW YOU THE MEDAL.

Sorry, Chicago.

NYAH, NYAH, NYAH.

Despite a previous commitment to hold the 1904 Games in the Windy City, the IOC changed course and opted for St. Louis, the better to take advantage with of an opportunity to host the sporting competitions at the **St. Luis World's Fair.**

The Whole World Was Watching

An embryonic Olympic movement strove dutifully to create itself in St. Louis:

THE GAMES WENT ON FOR FOUR AND A HALF MONTHS ... BUT ONLY *TWELVE NATIONS* SHOWED UP.

THESE WERE THE FIRST GAMES AT WHICH GOLD, SILVER, AND BRONZE *MEDALS* WERE AWARDED TO HONOR FIRST, SECOND, AND THIRD-PLACE FINISHES, RESPECTIVELY.

WINNER USED TO GET LAURELS AND TROPIES.

TOM KIELY OF IRELAND WON THE FIRST *DECATHLON*.

WORLD'S FAIR ORGANIZERS PROMOTED LOTS OF SUPPOSEDLY "OLYMPIC" ATHLETIC EVENTS DURING THIS FAIR. MOST OF THESE WERE LATER *DISCREDITED* BY THE IOC.

HELLO. I'M *WORLD'S GREATEST ATHLETE* NUMBER ONE.

Golden moments....

American athletes overwhelmed the Olympics, in part because international travel problems related to the Russo-Japanese War kept many foreign athletes away. U.S. athletes snagged 79 gold medals; the nations that tied for second place (Gerrnany, Cuba, and Canada) managed only four ... American Archie Hahn won gold medals in the 60-meter, 100-meter, and 200-meter races ... Swimmer Emil Rausch of Germany accounted for three of his country's four gold medals ... Tom Kiely of Ireland won the first decathlon, a ten-event track and field supercompetition then known as the "All-Around Championship" ... Zoltan Halmay won two gold medals in swimming for Hungary ... More than half of the events featured only American competitors ... Two years later, as a concession to the Greeks (who wanted the Games help permanently in their country), a round of "intercalated" off-year Games were held in Athens. These contests are no longer recognized as modern Olympic competitions.

21

1908: London Calling

Yet another marathon controversy descended on the 1908 Games ... this one in the presence of royalty. Italian runner **Dorando Pietri** staggered into the stadium for the final lap of what looked like a legitimate gold-metal performance. Problem was, the previous 26 miles had left Pietri exhausted, confused and disoriented. He no longer knew where he was going.

Helpful track officials steered Pietri in the right direction. It wasn't enough help, though. Pietri collapsed. Not once, but several times. Every time he came to, he was more clueless than before about where the finish line was. Finally, exasperated Olympic officials picked him up and carried him across the finish line. The excuse offered by Pietri's helpers (they feared he "might die in the very presence of the Queen") was not enough to snag the gold for the Italian. He was disqualified.

The gold medal in the marathon went, for the second straight Olympics, to the person initially thought to have finished second. (This time, the winner-by-default was John Hayes of the United States.)

> I'M A *GUY!* I'M NOT ABOUT TO STOP AND ASK FOR *DIRECTIONS!*

Ever watch the U.S. Olympic Team enter the stadium during the opening ceremonies? Unlike other groups of athletes, the Americans don't dip their flag to the host nation's head of state. How come? Well, you hear all kinds of explanations nowadays for this apparent breach of etiquette, but the snub originated in 1908 at the London Olympics. U.S. flagbearer Martin Sheridan refused to dip the American flag to the Queen. Sheridan, who was of Irish descent, objected to the English occupation of Ireland.

The best-laid plans ...

> THERE'S BEEN A SLIGHT CHANGE IN THE *SCHEDULE.*

The 1908 Olympics had originally been slated to take place in Rome ... but the eruption, in 1906, of Mt. Vesuvius forced a change of plans.

The Real Deal

ATHLETES MARCHED INTO THE OLYMPIC STADIUM BEARING THE **FLAG** OF THEIR COUNTRY.

THESE GAMES BEGAN THE **MODERN CYCLE** OF FOUR-YEAR OLYMPIADS.

NO MIXING OLYMPIC EVENTS WITH OTHER EVENTS.
NO CONCESSIONS TO OUTSIDE PROMOTERS.
NO **EMBARRASSING** SHORTAGES OF FOREIGN NATIONS.

IN LONDON, THE GAMES TOOK **CENTER STAGE!**

Golden moments....

Despite being disqualified in the Marathon, Pietri was given a special gold cup to honor his athletic spirit .... The advantage of the hosting nation, though not quite as surrealistic as in 1904 in St. Louis, was still pronounced: British athletes won 56 gold medals, while the Americans came in second with twelve ... Oscar Swahn of Sweden captured the gold medal in running deer shooting. He was 60 years old at the time, which meant he had established a record for the oldest competitor ever to win a gold medal. He topped his achievement when he snagged another gold as a 72-year old in 1920 in Antwerp as part of the Swedish team ... American Ray Ewry won his third consecutive gold in the standing long jump. He ended up winning a total of eight gold medals in the 1900, 1904, and 1908 games.

1912: The Jim Thorpe Show

SEEMS LIKE WHATEVER THEY GIVE, THEY FIND A WAY TO *TAKE BACK.*

Stockholm hosted the Games in 1912. What Games they were! American **Jim Thorpe** grabbed the spotlight with decisive gold medals in the pentathlon *and* the decathlon. Thorpe won nine of the fifteen sub-events in those two competitions outright, and left little doubt in anyone's mind that he was the best all-around competitor of the Games. After winning his medals, Thorpe had an audience with the King, who looked him in the eye and announced, **"You, sir, are the greatest athlete in the world."**

Neither Thorpe nor the King knew that another contest lay ahead of the great American-Indian competitor, one more daunting than any foot race, discus throw, or long jump. Thorpe had played semipro baseball for $25 a week in 1909 and 1910, and was apparently unaware that, under the strict Olympic rules of the time, this made him a professional athlete. His medals were stripped in 1913, despite protests from the Americans. Thorpe went on to win fame as a pro baseball player in the U.S., and was the subject of the classic Hollywood biopic *Jim Thorpe: All-American*. His medals were restored, posthumously, in 1982.

This was the first time that athletes representing all five continents (Europe, Africa, the Americas, Asia, and Australia) symbolized in the multicolored Olympic rings actually participated in the Olympic Games. (Antarctica was not considered a continent, and North and South America were combined.)

Scandalous!

WIMPY *AMERICANS...*

The 1912 Olympics were the first in which women are permitted to compete in the swimming events. No American women did so, however. U.S. policies prohibited women from taking part in any contest requiring them to appear in public wiithout long skirts.

Plot Twists in Stockholm

Sudden shifts of fate and close finishes marked the 1912 Olympics:

SWEDISH OFFICIALS UNEXPECTEDLY **BANNED BOXING** EVENTS FOR THESE OLYMPICS.

PORTUGUESE MARATHON RUNNER FRANCISCO LAZARO **COLLAPSED** DURING THE RACE, AND DIED THE NEXT DAY.

THIS WAS THE FIRST TIME **ELECTRIC TIMING SYSTEMS** WERE USED IN THE OLYMPIC GAMES.

 THAT CAME IN HANDY.

Golden moments....

Ralph Craig of the United States (above) won the 200 meters by one-tenth of a second ...Finnish long-distance runner Hannes Kolehmaine snagged three gold medals and a silver medal.... Matthew McGrath of the United States won the hammer throw ... Swedish athletes finished second to the United States, the first time since 1896 that a host country had not secured the most first-place finishes ... Konstantinos Tskilitiras was the standing long jump champion ...Henri Anspach of Belgium took the gold in fencing ... Sarah "Fanny" Durack of Australia became the first woman to win a gold medal in swimming by virtue of her first-place finish in the 100-meter freestyle ...These games were the last to feature "truly" gold medals. Subsequent Olympics would instead give victors medals composed primarily of other metals (generally silver) and coated with gold.

1916: The Olympics That Weren't

A **WINTER SPORTS WEEK,** AMONG OTHER INTRIGUING INNOVATIONS, HAD BEEN INCORPORATED INTO PLANS FOR THE 1916 OLYMPIC GAMES IN BERLIN ...

BUT.

Something unexpected happened along the way, something massive, something that took organizers, athletes, and indeed just about everyone else on earth by surprise ..., namely ....

The Great War.

The conflict we now know as "World War I" caught the IOC unawares. It destroyed more, and lasted longer, than anyone had anticipated. Even after it began in 1914, plans for the Berlin games had continued as though the hostilities would pass quickly. They didn't.

ARMISTICE FINALLY CAME IN 1918, AFTER FOUR YEARS OF BRUTAL, BLOODY AND OFTEN MYSTIFYINGLY COMPLEX CONFLICT.

YAY!

SO:

THE WAR WAS **OVER** ...

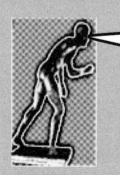

... AND THE OLYMPIC MOVEMENT, LIKE A **RUNNER** WHO STUMBLES BRIEFLY ON AN UNEXPECTED OBSTACLE, WAS BACK ON ITS FEET AGAIN.

27

1920: The Antwerp Allies

WHAT A *FINNISH!*

Okay, so the roster of the 1920 games in Antwerp didn't *exactly* live up to the global-brotherhood ethic that had launched the modern Olympic movement ... but hey, there was still that whole Great War thing to sort through. People were still reeling from the conflict today known as World War I when the time came to determine who was on (and off) he list of participating nations. Thus, pacifist dream or no pacifist dream, the athletes of Turkey, Hungary, Bulgaria, Austria, and Germany did not make the cut, basically because their governments were still regarded as bad guys from the last war. Finland made the list, though, which was fortunate for **Paavlo Nurmi.**

The great long-distance runner snagged gold medals in the 10,000-meter, 8,000-meter cross country, and 8,000 meter cross country team events. Even greater accomplishments on the Olympic stage were to come from the "Flying Finn" in 1924.

Great Britain's Philip Noel-Baker won the silver medal for his effort in the 1500-meter dash. Thirty-nine years later, in 1959, he would win the Nobel Peace Prize. Noel-Baker remains the only individual to win both an Olympic medal and a Nobel Prize.

The Olympic Oath

WE SWEAR: WE WILL TAKE PART IN THE OLYMPIC GAMES IN A SPIRIT OF CHIVALRY, FOR THE HONOR OF OUR COUNTRY AND THE GLORY OF SPORT.

Antwerp's Games marked the debut of the oath above. It would be revised in later years to refer instead to the "honor of our team," and, eventually, to include a promise to reject doping. Belgian fencer Victor Boin (above) was the first to make the oath formally during opening ceremonies.

To Everything There Is a Season

Antwerp helped to pave the way for the Winter Olympics:

TODAY, WE THINK OF THE EARLIEST MODERN OLYMPICS CONTESTS AS "SUMMER" EVENTS ... BUT SOME, LIKE THIS ONE, FEATURED *"WINTER"* COMPETITIONS, TOO.

ICE HOCKEY, FOR INSTANCE, MADE ITS DEBUT AT ANTWERP.

FIGURE SKATING SHOWED UP FOR THE SECOND TIME. (THE FIRST HAD BEEN LONDON IN 1908.)

Golden moments....

The Belgian team hit the bull's-eye, with six gold medals in the archery competition .... The British scored gold in the tug-of-war competition, which was never to reappear in any future Olympic competition .... Alfred Neuland of Estonia took one of the gold medals in weightlifting, a sport that had been absent from the Olympics since 1904, but was, from this point forward, to emerge as one of the signature events of the Games ... Gustav Dyrssen of Sweden took the gold medal in the modern pentathlon, which had debuted in 1912. The modern pentathlon features sub-competitions in fencing, pistol shooting, equestrian jumping, freestyle swimming, and cross-country running.

1924: Winter Debuts ... Kind Of

Chamonix, in Haute-Savoie, France, like Paris before it, hosted an event that presented something of an identity crisis. This event is only *retroactively* certain of having been an Olympic competition.

At the time the games played out, the athletes participating in it were under the impression that they're taking part in an "International Winter Sports Week." After years of debate, the IOC hadn't yet figured out whether it wanted a formal Olympic event devoted exclusively to winter sports. These games were, however, eventually declared to have been the first Winter Olympics.

OKAY, I *GIVE UP* ... IS IT THE OLYMPICS, OR ISN'T IT?

BEATS ME...

No home advantage for the host nation this time -- the Norwegians and the Finns dominate the proceedings, while the French manage a ninth-place finish with three total medals.

Their game, their rink, their medal.

NO, IT'S NOT A MISPRINT.

FINAL CUMULATIVE SCORE:

CANADA: 110 ...
EVERYBODY ELSE: 3!

The Canadian ice hockey team went 4-0 in its qualifying round, crushed all available competition, and cruised to one of the most decisive gold medals in the history of the Olympics.

In the Beginning ...

Intriguing newcomers and lopsided victories marked the first Winter Games:

NORWAY'S ELEVEN-YEAR-OLD FIGURE SKATER **SONJA HENIE** FINISHED LAST, BUT WAS A CROWD FAVORITE. SHE WOULD MORE THAN MAKE UP FOR HER MODEST SHOWING IN LATER GAMES.

CANADA'S GOLD-MEDAL WINNING ICE HOCKEY TEAM BEGAN AN OLYMPIC **DYNASTY** .

NORWAY AND FINLAND WON **28** TOTAL MEDALS, OUT OF A POSSIBLE 49.

Golden moments....

American Charles Jewtraw comes in first in the in the 500-meter speed skating event, and thus secures the very first Winter Olympics gold medal .... American Anders Haugen is declared the fourth-place finisher in the ski-jump competition; Thorleif Haug of Norway is awarded the bronze. Half a century later, the IOC acknowledges that a scoring error deprived Haugen of the medal he actually won, declares the similarly-named Haug the fourth-place finisher, and bestows a bronze on Haugen. ... Speed skater Clas Thunberg of Norway wins three gold medals ... Gillis Grafstrom, who won the figure-skating medal in Antwerp in 1920, won the gold here as well.

31

1924: Stars on Display

The Paris Olympics of 1924 led to not one, but two, major Hollywood legends. The first involved swimmer **Johnny Weissmuller,** who snagged gold medals in the 100-meter freestyle, the 400-meter freestyle, and the 4 x 100-meter freestyle relay, with a bronze in water polo thrown in for good measure. Weissmuller, one of the greatest swimmers of his era, later found fame and fortune in Tinseltown playing **Tarzan.**

The other movie legend? Well, it involved British runners Harold Abrahams and Eric Liddell, who won gold in the 100 meters and 400 meters, respectively, at this Olympics. No, they didn't go on to careers as actors ... but their stories do form the basis of the 1981 film *Chariots of Fire*. The picture took considerable liberties with the facts. In reality, Liddell, a devout churchgoer, knew long before the Olympics started that his signature event, the 100-meter dash, was scheduled for the Sabbath; he practiced assiduously for the 400. Poetic license aside, the film stands, in our humble opinion, as as the finest picture about the Olympics ever made. It won the Oscar for best picture of the year, which is as close as Hollywood gets to giving out a gold medal.

JANE!
BOY!
ME WIN *THREE GOLD MEDALS!*

Sidney Hinds, a U.S. rifleman, notched a perfect 50 in the free-frifle team event. **Impressed? Not yet, you're not.** *During his shooting round,* Hinds was accidentally shot in the foot by a Belgian opponent who dropped his weapon. He kept shooting (the target, not the Belgian) and helped his team win the gold.

Once more for old time's sake.

DEJA VU, MAN...

Reportedly, Paris got the nod as the host city of the 1924 because retiring IOC president Baron de Coubertin wanted to see the games in his home country one last time.

1920 HERO *PAAVO NURMI* OF FINLAND MAKES AN EVEN MORE EMPHATIC STATEMENT HERE, WINNING FIVE GOLD MEDALS.

NURMI'S VICTORIES IN THE 1500-METER AND 5000-METER RACES *BOGGLE THE MIND.*

TOP THAT!

HE WINS THOSE TWO RACES *WITHIN AN HOUR* OF EACH OTHER, SETTING A *NEW WORLD RECORD* WITH EACH RACE!

Golden moments....

Now-legendary runner Nurmi (above) stole the spotlight with an Olympics for the ages, netting five gold medals; teammate Ville Ritola snagged four ... French fencer Roger Ducret won three gold medals ... The Americans easily led the overall count, winning a total of 99 medals, 45 of which were gold. In a distant second place were the Finns, with a total of 38 medals, 13 of which were gold. The Olympic motto Citius, Altius, Fortius (Faster, Higher, Stronger) made its debut at these Games.

As though hoping to settle the matter once and for all, the IOC issued its formal definition of an "amateur" following these games. It read: "One who devotes himself to sport for sport's sake without deriving from it, directly or indirectly, the means of existence." The IOC defined a "professional" as "one who derives the means of existence entirely or partly from sport." The guidelines formally exclude "professionals" from the Olympics, and include in that category athletes who are compensated for taking time off from work.

1928: Sonja in St. Moritz

1924's adorable last-place kid became 1928's winter heroine, as teenager Sonja Henie of Norway took the gold medal in figure skating. The triumph at St. Moritz followed Henie's victory at the World Figure Skating Championships the previous year.

Henie would go on to win more world and Olympic titles than any other female figure skater. Her innovative costuming and choreography are seen today as landmark events in the history of her sport.

As though all of that weren't enough, she would eventually become a major Hollywood star ... but not before snagging gold medals in two more stellar Winter Olympics (1932 and 1936).

WATCH OUT, WORLD ... HERE I COME!

Unseasonably warm weather was a major problem at St. Moritz, forcing officials to reschedule some events and abandon others (such as the 10,000-meter speed skating race) entirely.

Flying high.

FINALLY ... LIFTOFF!

The sport of ski jumping made its debut as an official Olympic event in 1924. Jacob Tullin Thams of Norway took the gold.

The Winter Games Get Hot

The winter contests started to pick up serious momentum in St. Moritz:

25 NATIONS SHOWED UP FOR THE WINTER GAMES, COMPARED WITH 16 IN 1924.

ARGENTINA'S PARTICIPATION WAS THE FIRST BY ANY **SOUTHERN-HEMISPHERE** COUNTRY IN ANY OLYMPICS.

GILLIS GRAFSTROM WON HIS **THIRD CONSECUTIVE** GOLD MEDAL IN FIGURE SKATING. HIS FIRST HAD COME IN ANTWERP.

Golden moments....

Grafstrom, the men's gold-medal figure skater, served simultaneously as coach to Sonja Henie, the women's figure skating champion ... Bernt Evensen of Norway took three gold medals in the speed skating competitions ... To the surprise of absolutely no one, the Canadian squad took another gold in ice hockey, continuing a dominance of the sport that began in 1924... Teammates Johan Grotumsbraten and Ole Hegge of Norway finished one-two in the 18-km cross-country skiing event ... The US teams won both the gold and silver medals in the bobsled event.

1928: The Flame Lights the Way

WHY DIDN'T WE THINK OF THIS *TWENTY-FIVE HUNDRED YEARS AGO?*

The 1928 Amsterdam Games were the first to feature the now-iconic Olympic Flame.. (You probably thought it was one of those ceremonies the ancient Greeks came up with, didn't you?)

The lighting of the Olympic flame has since become one of the great rituals of the Games, with each new opening ceremony incorporating some new "twist" on the ceremonial event. The best-known tradition, that of having a series of athletes transfer the flame by relay would not emerge until 1936, in Berlin.

After spending a decade in exile as punishment for their government's role in World War I, the German team returned to the Olympic fold in 1928, winning 10 gold medals and 31 overall. Nowadays, it's hard to imagine a government's policies resulting in the punishment of its prospective Olympic athletes. Then again, it was hard to imagine the Olympics without Germany in the first place.

The return of the Germans wasn't the only concession to, um, reality on display in Amsterdam. These games were the first to be explicitly designated as "summer" games, in order to distinguish them from the now-official "winter" contests. Retroactively, the warm-weather Olympic competitions of 1896, 1900, 1904, 1908, 1912, 1916, 1920, and 1924 are unofficially regarded as "summer" games. Their official name, however, remains "Games of the Insert-Fancy-Looking-Roman-Numeral-Here Olympiad."

The General weighs in.

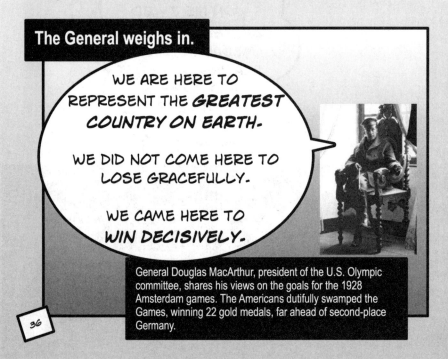

WE ARE HERE TO REPRESENT THE *GREATEST COUNTRY ON EARTH.*

WE DID NOT COME HERE TO LOSE GRACEFULLY.

WE CAME HERE TO *WIN DECISIVELY.*

General Douglas MacArthur, president of the U.S. Olympic committee, shares his views on the goals for the 1928 Amsterdam games. The Americans dutifully swamped the Games, winning 22 gold medals, far ahead of second-place Germany.

Welcome to the Modern World

Amsterdam made concessions to tradition ... and to the 20th century:

TO COMMEMORATE ITS HISTORIC ROLE IN THE ANCIENT GAMES, **GREECE** WAS PERMITTED TO LEAD THE PARADE OF NATIONS DURING THE OPENING CEREMONIES.

DESPITE **OBJECTIONS FROM THE POPE,** WOMEN COMPETED IN GYMNASTICS AND TRACK AND FIELD EVENTS FOR THE FIRST TIME.

ATHLETES FROM **28 DIFFERENT COUNTRIES** WON MEDALS ... A NEW HIGH.

THESE GAMES FEATURED A CORPORATE SPONSOR: **COCA-COLA.**

Golden moments....

Paavo Nurmi picked up his ninth gold medal ... The American men's track and field squad took eight first-place fnishes ... India took the field hockey championship ... Mikio Oda of Japan took the triple long jump competition ... During a quarterfinal, Australian rower Henry Pearce noticed a flock of ducks passing in front of his boat. He dutifully stopped rowing, and continued once they had passed in front of him. He ended up winning both the quarterfinal race and the gold medal for individual rowing ... The United States took 56 total medals, 22 of them gold, to lead the field in both categories.

1932: The Big Chill

I KNEW I COULD GET **AIRBORNE!**

The Depression didn't keep Billy Fiske from leading the American four-man bobsled team to a first-place finish. (He had also shared in a team bobsled gold in St. Moritz) Fiske, a born extrovert and adventurer, was always on the lookout for a challenge.

Disgusted by Hitler's military aggression, Fiske decided to join the British Royal Air Force in 1939 to defend the British people. He died in action in 1940 while engaged in a mission to push back a Nazi attack.

So it was that Fiske, an American, became a national hero in England, and the national four-man bobsled trophy now bears his name.

The Games had been scheduled to be held in Big Pines, California, but weather conditions forced a shift to Lake Placid, New York. Lake Placid was a tiny community of less than 4000 inhabitants, and the Depression had taken its toll on the local, national, and global economy. Fundraising was a challenge. The president of the organizing committee, Dr. Godfrey Dewey, made a substantial land donation that enabled Oympic officials to build a bobsled run.

ANYBODY IN THE MARKET FOR A **GOLD MEDAL?**

Wall Street freaks out; the post-crash games go on.

In stark contrast to the prosperity that drove Olympic events in 1928, the Lake Placid games played out in an atmosphere of economic uncertainty. Speed skater Irving Jaffee of the U.S. won two gold medals at Lake Placid ... but, out of a job, was soon forced to pawn them for $3500. He never recovered them.

38

Tight Budgets, Big Stars

Some major names were on display at the 1932 Lake Placid Olympics:

SONJA HENIE WON ANOTHER GOLD MEDAL IN FIGURE SKATING.

THE **CANADIAN ICE HOCKEY DYNASTY** CONTINUED UNABATED.

WHAT A CAMPAIGN OPPORTUNITY!

GOVERNOR **FRANKLIN D. ROOSEVELT** OFFICIALLY OPENED THE GAMES. LATER THAT YEAR, HE WOULD WIN THE U.S. PRESIDENCY.

ANDREE AND PIERRE BRUNET DEFENDED THE GOLD THEY HAD WON IN PAIRS FIGURE SKATING IN 1928.

Golden moments....

Sven Utterstrom of Sweden won the 18-km cross-country skiing event; Veli Saarinen of Finland came in first in the 59-km race ...Birger Ruud of Norway picked up the win in the ski jumping event .... Lake Placid resident Jack Shea picked up two gold medals, helping the US to secure a first-place finish in both total medals (6) and gold medals (12).

WHEN FDR OPENED THE 1932 GAMES, LAKE PLACID WAS AN ANONYMOUS VILLAGE. IT EVENTUALLY HOSTED ANOTHER WINTER OLYMPICS (1980) AND BECAME AN INTERNATIONAL WINTER SPORTS AND MOUNTANEERING DESTINATION.

1932: The Other Babe

BABE *RUTH?*

WHO THE HELL IS BABE *RUTH?*

The athlete count was down, way down, compared to the 1928 Games in Amsterdam. That was primarily due to global economic woes. Yet those competitors who actually did make their way to Los Angeles put on a show that gave the world something besides the Depression to focus on. In the process, they made some serious history.

Chief history-maker: track and field star **Babe Didrikson,** who had, the previous year, set five world records in a single day. In L.A., she secured medals in the javelin throw and the hurdles, and would have won the gold in the high jump if the judges hadn't had a problem with her unorthodox jumping style. (Didrikson went over the bar headfirst.) Didrikson's athletic gifts were astonishingly diverse, and she is generally reckoned as the most versatile female athlete in history, and certainly one of the greatest. In addition to her track and field exploits, she was a superb basketball player, although no women's Olympic basketball event existed for her to enter in 1932.

At the time she won big in Los Angeles, Didrikson had not yet competed seriously in the sport that would win her the most acclaim of her astonishing career. She emerged as America's leading female golfer in the 1940s.

Swedish horseman Bertill Handstrom looked like he had wrapped up second place in the individual dressage event, until judges ruled that he had been making illegal vocal sounds to encourage his horse. Handstrom's explanation .. that the noises had actually emanated from his saddle ... did not impress the authorities.

California's second gold rush.

SURE, WE WANT THE OLYMPICS!

No other city put in a bid to host the 932 Olympics, probably because, at a time of global economic crisis, the (usually unprofitable) Olympic Games seemed like an unffortable luxury. L.A. had the last laugh. These Games reportedly turned a $1 million profit.

Tight Budgets, Big Stars

Some major names were on display at the 1932 Lake Placid Olympics:

THE **CANADIAN ICE HOCKEY DYNASTY** CONTINUED UNABATED.

SONJA HENIE WON ANOTHER GOLD MEDAL IN FIGURE SKATING.

WHAT A CAMPAIGN OPPORTUNITY!

GOVERNOR **FRANKLIN D. ROOSEVELT** OFFICIALLY OPENED THE GAMES. LATER THAT YEAR, HE WOULD WIN THE U.S. PRESIDENCY.

ANDREE AND PIERRE BRUNET DEFENDED THE GOLD THEY HAD WON IN PAIRS FIGURE SKATING IN 1928.

Golden moments....

Sven Utterstrom of Sweden won the 18-km cross-country skiing event; Veli Saarinen of Finland came in first in the 59-km race ...Birger Ruud of Norway picked up the win in the ski jumping event .... Lake Placid resident Jack Shea picked up two gold medals, helping the US to secure a first-place finish in both total medals (6) and gold medals (12).

WHEN FDR OPENED THE 1932 GAMES, LAKE PLACID WAS AN ANONYMOUS VILLAGE. IT EVENTUALLY HOSTED ANOTHER WINTER OLYMPICS (1980) AND BECAME AN INTERNATIONAL WINTER SPORTS AND MOUNTANEERING DESTINATION.

1932: The Other Babe

BABE *RUTH?*

WHO THE HELL IS BABE *RUTH?*

The athlete count was down, way down, compared to the 1928 Games in Amsterdam. That was primarily due to global economic woes. Yet those competitors who actually did make their way to Los Angeles put on a show that gave the world something besides the Depression to focus on. In the process, they made some serious history.

Chief history-maker: track and field star **Babe Didrikson,** who had, the previous year, set five world records in a single day. In L.A., she secured medals in the javelin throw and the hurdles, and would have won the gold in the high jump if the judges hadn't had a problem with her unorthodox jumping style. (Didrikson went over the bar headfirst.) Didrikson's athletic gifts were astonishingly diverse, and she is generally reckoned as the most versatile female athlete in history, and certainly one of the greatest. In addition to her track and field exploits, she was a superb basketball player, although no women's Olympic basketball event existed for her to enter in 1932.

At the time she won big in Los Angeles, Didrikson had not yet competed seriously in the sport that would win her the most acclaim of her astonishing career. She emerged as America's leading female golfer in the 1940s.

Swedish horseman Bertill Handstrom looked like he had wrapped up second place in the individual dressage event, until judges ruled that he had been making illegal vocal sounds to encourage his horse. Handstrom's explanation .. that the noises had actually emanated from his saddle ... did not impress the authorities.

California's second gold rush.

SURE, WE WANT THE OLYMPICS!

No other city put in a bid to host the 932 Olympics, probably because, at a time of global economic crisis, the (usually unprofitable) Olympic Games seemed like an unffortable luxury. L.A. had the last laugh. These Games reportedly turned a $1 million profit.

You Ain't Seen Nothin' Yet ...

The 1932 Games featured stuff had never been seen at the Olympics:

THIS OLYMPICS MARKED THE FIRST USE OF THE *VICTORY PODIUM*.

AND THE FIRST CONSTRUCTION OF AN *OLYMPIC VILLAGE*.

AND THE FIRST TIME SOMEBODY GOT A MEDAL FOR *LOSING* EVERY EVENT.

(THAT WOULD BE THE U.S. FIELD HOCKEY TEAM, WHICH DROPPED BOTH ITS CONTESTS, BUT STILL FINISHED *THIRD*. THERE WERE ONLY THREE NATIONS COMPETING.)

Golden moments....

Johan Gabriel Oxenstiema of Sweden won the gold in the modern pentathlon ... In one of the stranger chapters of Olympic history, Poland's Stanislawa Walasiewicz came in first in the women's 100 meters event. Forty-eight years later, after her death, an autopsy revealed that she carried both male and female chromosomes, possesed male sex organs, and was technically ineligible to compete in this Olympics. The condition is technically known as "intersex." As of this writing, her status as a gold-medal winner has not been revoked ....The United States won 41 gold medals, and 103 overall, to lead the field .... Finnish superstar Paavo Nurmi was declared a professional and was thus barred from competing ... U.S. swimmer Buster Crabbe, later to win fame on the silver screen as Flash Gordon, picked up the gold medal in the 400-meter men's freestyle.

1936: Bavarian Rhapsody

Home team favorite **Franz Pfnur** of Germany took the first medal in alpine (a.k.a downhill) skiing, but his victory was not entirely without controversy. Ski instructors were regarded as professionals, which means that many aspiring competitors on the Austrian and Swiss teams were ineligible to compete. Those two nations boycotted the event. Germany doesn't, though, which leads to the German medal.

The ski-instructor controversy exposes still more fault lines in the IOC's guidelines for answering the persistent and ever-vexing question: *"Okay, I give up: who counts as a professional?"*

Imagining they've solved the problem, authorities simply opt not to hold the downhill skiing event in the 1940 Olympics. Unbeknownst to the Men in Suits, there will *be* no Olympics in 1940. The world will, alas, have more pressing questions to resolve. (But alpine will return in 1948.)

The Games take place in two southern Bavarian towns, Garmisch and Partenkirchen. Actually, make that one town. German leader Adolf Hitler forced the two to unite as a single municipality, despite 1100 years of history as neighbors, in order to better fulfill their duties as host city to this Olympics. The resulting town, Garmich-Partenkirchen, operates as a single entity to this day.

Norway's hero.

Ivar Ballangrud of Norway laid his claim to the title of greatest speed skater in the world by winning three gold medals and a silver in these Olympics. He narrowly lost the chance for a fourth gold to Norwegian teammate Charles Mathiesen.

Adolf's Games?

THE **NAZIS** DREW A LOT OF CRITICISM AS THEY HOSTED THEIR FIRST OLYMPICS.

HEIL WHO?

AN AMERICAN–LED EFFORT TO **BOYCOTT** THE OLYMPICS AND THE NAZI REGIME FELL FLAT.

SPEED SKATER JACK SHEA, WHO HAD WON A GOLD MEDAL IN LAKE PLACID IN 1932, DECIDED TO **SKIP THE GAMES** RATHER THAN ENDORSE THE NAZI REGIME IN ANY WAY.

Golden moments....

Norway led the way at this Olympics, with seven gold medals and fifteen overall ... Jewish hockey player Rudi Ball, the only Jew on the German Olympic team, could not manage to lead the German squad to a medal. Ball's presence at these Olympics was widely seen as a P.R. move by Nazi organizers eager to soften international criticism of vitriolic Nazi anti-Semitism ... Karl Shafer of Austria took the men's figure skating medal ... After dominating yet another Olympic figure skating competition, and securing her third consecutive gold medal, Sonja Henie turned pro after this competition, began touring in her own ice show, and launched her career as a Hollywood actress.

43

> I'M RUNNING INTO THE FUTURE ... AND NO WAY THE PAST CAN BEAT THAT.

The 1936 Summer Olympics were

held in Berlin. German organizers envisioned the games as a global propaganda opportunity for the Nazi regime ... and a vindication of Adolf Hitler's philosophy of "Aryan superiority," which held that Jews and ethnic Africans (among others) were physically and mentally inferior to German athletes.

The biggest news of the competition came when Hitler chose to shake hands only with German medal winners. Reportedly, this was to avoid having to make physical contact with African-American champions like Cornelius Johnson, who won the gold medal in the high jump, and **Jesse Owens**,(left) who stormed his way to gold medals in the 100-meter sprint, the long jump, the 200 meter dash, and the 4x100 meter relay. Owens's was among the truly great Olympic achievements. At the time, reperters made a big deal of Hitler's apparent snub of the US athletes ... but they ignored equally grave indignities back home. After the Games, Owens had to ride a freight elevator to attend a reception held in his honor at New York's posh, but still segregated, Waldorf-Astoria hotel. Turns out Nazi Germany wasn't the only country with ugly ideas about "racial purity."

No medals for Eleanor Holm, who had scored gold in the 1932 swimming competition. She was tossed off the U.S. team for unbecoming behavior during the ocean voyage to Europe. Holm reportedly spent a fair amount of her shipboard time partying: shooting craps, getting drunk, and swearing robustly while her head protruded through a porthole.

Megalomaniac, genocidal madman ... and peacenik?

German Chancellor Adolf Hitler welcomes the Olympic flame ... before he launched the Holocaust and invaded Poland:

> "(THE OLYMPIC ATHLETE) HELPS TO CONNECT THE COUNTRIES IN THE *SPIRIT OF PEACE.* THAT'S WHY THE OLYMPIC FLAME SHOULD NEVER DIE."

Maybe he was being, you know, ironic.

The World Gathers in Berlin

THE FILM *OLYMPIA*, DIRECTED BY NAZI PROPAGANDIST LENI RIEFENSTAHL, WAS THE FIRST FULL-LENGTH FILM DOCUMENTING AN OLYMPIC COMPETITION.

ANTI-FASCISTS PLANNED A COUNTER-OLYMPICS IN SPAIN MEANT TO PROTEST NAZI PROPAGANDA CONNECTED WITH THIS EVENT, BUT THEY HAD TO CANCEL DUE TO THE OUTBREAK OF THE SPANISH CIVIL WAR.

THESE GAMES MARKED THE FIRST TIME THE *OLYMPIC FLAME* WAS PASSED BY RELAY.

AS WITH THE WINTER GAMES, A PLANNED *BOYCOTT* PROTESTING THE NAZI SPONSORSHIP OF THE GAMES FAILED TO GET OFF THE GROUND.

Golden moments....

German Toni Merkens won the cycling medal despite fouling a competitor ... Swimmer Rie Mastenbroek of the Netherlands won three gold medals and a silver ... a disputed soccer (football) final saw Peru defeat Austria 4-2, but the result was thrown out due to the interference of Peruvian fans after the fourth Peruvian goal. The government of Peru refused to replay the game, and no gold medal was awarded. Austria took the silver.

45

1940: Flames of Destruction

A vast global conflict engulfed the globe.
The 1940 Winter games were to have been mounted in Sappro, Japan, but Japan withdrew its offer to host the games with the commencement of the Second Sino-Japanese War in 1937. For a time, it seemed as though the Winter games might be held in either Switzerland or Germany, but the invasion of Poland in 1939 caused the cancellation of the winter contests, and, eventually, the projected 1940 Summer Olympics in Helsinki, Finland.

1944: And the War Rages on ...

The bloody conflict continued.

The 1944 Winter Olympics, which had been assigned to Italy before the outbreak of World War II, were canceled, as were the 1944 Summer Olympics that had been awarded to London. Finally, a devastated Germany surrendered in April of 1945, and Japan did the same after the United States dropped Atomic bombs on the cities of Hiroshima and Nagasaki. The level of destruction exceeded even that of the Great War ... but the Olympic movement's response, once the fighting stopped, was the same : Mount the next Games. *The world set its sights on St. Moritz in 1948.*

1948: Picking Up the Pieces

BUTTON, BUTTON, WHO'S GOT THE GOLDEN BUTTON?

The first Olympic Games in twelve years took place against the familiar backdrop of St. Moritz, Switzerland, the site of the 1928 Olympics. Fortuitously, St. Moritz had been left undamaged by World War II.

Once again, in the aftermath of war, the athletes of aggressive nations were punished for the decisions of their government. Germany and Japan were not on the guest list. Former Axis power Italy was on hand to compete, raising any number of touchy questions, but such inconsistencies were, as usual, left to the bureaucrats.

The talk of the Games was U.S. figure skater **Dick Button,** who pulled off the first double axel in competition to defeat riveal Hans Gerschwiler. Button was only eighteen at the time. He went on to a long and successful career as a broadcast skating commentator.

Skeleton (a head-first variation on the luge) makes its return to the Winter Games after a twenty--year absence. Nino Bibbia of Itraly takes the gold, but that's not what got everyone talking. What was truly remarkable was American John Heaton's second-place finish. He had won the silver in the same event at the *1928* St. Moritz games!

Five times as much frostbite.

GIVE ME A @#$% BREAK.

Presumably on the theory that the biathlon, which combines target shooting with cross country skiing, isn't difficult enough, the winter pentathlon was presented as a demonstration sport in 1948. It featured five sub-competitions: cross-country skiing, shooting, downhill skiing, fencing, and horse riding. it never became an official Olympic sport.

Back on Track

After a long wait, the world's athletes resumed the quest for gold:

OVERZEALOUS AMERICANS WERE BARRED FROM ANY HOCKEY MEDAL, BECAUSE THEY SENT **TWO COMPETING HOCKEY SQUADS** TO THE GAMES.

NORWAY TOOK ALL THREE GOLD MEDALS IN SKI JUMPING.

BARBARA ANN SCOTT OF **CANADA** TOOK THE GOLD IN WOMEN'S FIGURE SKATING.

Golden moments....

Switzerland took first and second in the two-man bobsled event ... Sweden took all three first-place finishes in the cross-country skiing events .. Canada resumed its customary spot at the top of the hockey proceedings, winning its fourth gold medal in the last five Olympics ... Gretchen Fraser of the United States took the gold medal in the women's alpine skiing event ... In a tight finish of national teams, Norway, Sweden, and Switzerland each finished with ten total medals.

1948: London Resurgent

> NOW **THAT'S** WHAT I CALL A DUTCH TREAT!

Fanny Blankers-Koen was determined to make up for lost time.

The Dutch runner had represented her country at the 1936 Olympics in Berlin at the age of eighteen, but had not medaled. She later admitted that the highlight of those games, for her, had been securing the autograph of her hero Jesse Owens, the great American sprinter. She had dreamed of dominating an Olympcs competition in the way Owens had ... but then World War II had eliminated the Games that were scheduled during her prime running years.

At the age of thirty, having given birth to two children, and having reached a point when most female runners retired from the sport, Fanny decided to take her shot in London. She won four gold medals, in the 200 meters, the 100 metes, the 80 meter hurdles, and the 4 x 100 meter relay, thereby equaling the output of her idol, Jesse Owens. She was, at the time, the oldest woman competing in the Olympic track and field events.

Czech marksman Karoly Takacs took the gold medal in the rapid-fire pistol contest. Takacs was shooting left-handed ... of necessity, since his right hand, which he had favored from birth, had been disabled a decade earlier in a hand-grenade explosion.

Olympic turn-on.

> SORRY. NO INSTANT REPLAY.

The 1948 London Games are the first to be broadcast on home TV.

The Low-Budget Olympics

Times were tight in a London that was still recovering from war in 1948:

MUCH OF LONDON WAS STILL IN **RUINS** FROM THE BLITZ.

THE SIMILARLY WAR-RAVAGED **SOVIET UNION** WAS INVITED, BUT DID NOT ATTEND.

OPRGANIZERS WERE SO **SHORT ON CASH** THAT THEY HAD TO DOUSE THE OLYMPIC FLAME AT NIGHT.

Golden moments....

Marie Provaznikova of Czechoslovakia won the women's gymnastics event and promptly defected, citing a "lack of freedom" in her home country, which has been one of many that received a pro-Soviet government after the war ... Harold Sakata of the United States won a silver medal in weightlifting. He would go on to play the demented, hat-flinging villain Oddjob in the James Bond movie *Goldfinger* ...The American team won the basketball event, which was finally held indoors. (Poor weather had undermined the outdoor finals of the 1936 basketball competition.) ... Americans took a total of 84 medals, 38 of which were gold, to lead the field. A highlight for the US team was the victory of runner Bob Mathias in the marathon ... Hungarian fencer Ilona Elek successfully defended the gold medal she had won in Berlin in 1936.

1952: Oslo's Solo

Nineteen-year old American skiier Andrea Mead-Lawrence came out of nowhere at Oslo to win two gold medals in the women's alpine events. She captured the second medal in particularly breathtaking style, having fallen during her first run. Her second run down the mountain, however, was a full two seconds faster than anyone else's time, and Mead-Lawrence thus became the first American woman to win two gold medals in an alpine event.

In 1956, she narrowly missed an Olympic bronze medal in the grand slalom competition, falling just a tenth of a second behind the third-place finisher. Just four months earlier, Mead-Lawrence had given birth to her third child!

Mead-Lawrence's husband, skier David Lawrence, quickly learned that he was never to wish his wife "good luck" before she competed in an event. She always preferred to be told to "have fun."

THIS GIRL JUST WANTS TO HAVE *FUN!*

Oslo won the right to host the games and step into the global spotlight. Athletes representing thirty nations arrived in Norway to compete in these Games, the highest total thus far for a Winter Olympics. The Federal Republic of Germany was invited, and did attend, marking the first appearance of German athletes at the Olympics since 1936.

Peace, man.

LISTEN, ABOUT THOSE BERLIN GAMES ...

In addition to hosing the Winter Olympics, Oslo, Norway was, and is, the site of the ceremonies awarding the Nobel Peace Prize. The most recent winner at the time of these Games was union leader and concentration camp survivor Leon Jouhaux, a vocal opponent of fascism and a critic of the Nazi government that had staged the 1936 Berlin Games.

Home Ice Advantage

> THE OLYMPIC TORCH WAS IGNITED IN THE FIREPLACE OF NORWEGIAN SKIING LEGEND *SONDRE NORHEIM*...

> ... AND 94 SKIERS THEN **RELAYED** THE FLAME TO THE SITE OF THE GAMES.

> TRUCKIN' ...

> NORWEGIAN TRUCK DRIVER *HJALMAR ANDERSEN* (RIGHT) WON THREE SPEED SKATING MEDALS, AND THE NORWEGIAN TEAM LED THE OVERALL MEDAL COUNT.

Golden moments....

Italian Zeno Colo took the alpine skiing event ... Germany took gold medals in both the two-man and the four-man bobsled... In figure skating, Dick Button of the US successfully defended his 1948 gold medal, and Jeannette Altwegg of Great Britain took the ladies' gold. Germany's Paul and Ria Falk took the pairs figure skating title .... Arnfinn Bergmann of Norway overcame his countryman Torbjorn Falkanger to take the gold in ski jumping.

1952: The Finnish Line

Czech long-distance runner

Emil Zatopek won the biggest headlines at the summer Games, and, as the final event played out, also earned himself a unique accomplishment in track and field history, one that is unlikely to be challenged in any future Olympics.

Zatopek – winner of the 5,000-meter and 10,000-meter races – threw the dice and decided to enter the marathon, an event for which he had not trained, and in which he had never even competed. He won.

Given the level of competition, the sophisticated athletic regimens now in place in top national Olympic organizations, and the many resources available to contemporary marathon competitors, the chance of a rookie winning the 26.2-mile footrace in a contemporary Olympics seem remote indeed. But it happened in Helsinki – and, as a result, Zatopek's stellar Olympics will rank among the truly legendary athletic performances in history.

> MARATHON? WHAT'S A MARATHON?

Give thanks that you're not Vince Farrell, the referee in the France-Uruguay basketball game. As the game wound down, Farrell called fouls that resulted in so many foul-outs that the Uruguayans were only able to put three men on the court. He was later attacked by members of the losing Uruguay squad and their fans, some of whom appeared to disagree with Farrell's officiating style. They kicked him vigorously in the private parts. No, really.

Welcome, comrades.

> RED MUST WIN GOLD.

The Soviet government decides it's time to suit up, so athletes from the U.S.S.R. take part in the Olympics for the first time in four decades.

Helsinki Hurrah

> A LONG-RUNNING **COLD WAR** COMPETITION BETWEEN U.S. AND SOVIET RIVALS BEGAN WITH THESE OLYMICS.

> JOSY BARTHEL OF TINY **LUXEMBOURG** SEEMED TO COME OUT NOWHERE TO WIN THE MEN'S 1500 METERS.

> FINNISH OLYMPIC HERO **PAAVO NURMI** LIT THE OLYMPIC FLAME.

> HOT STUFF!

Golden moments....

Soviet gymnast Maria Gorokhovskaya wins seven medals, two gold and five silver, beginning a pattern of Russian excellence in the gymnastics competition that will outlive the Soviet Union itself. The Helsinki Games marked the first international gymnastics competition in which Soviet athletes took part .... American track star Bob Mathias successfully defended his 1948 gold medal in the decathlon ... The Americans narrowly eclipsed the Russians in the race for most overall medals (76-71), but finished with a comfortable lead over their Cold War rivals in total gold medals (40-22) ... Pal Adam Kovacs of Hungary took the gold medal in men's individual sabre fencing, helping tiny Hungary to secure an astonishing third-place finish in the race for most overall medals.

Avery Brundage assumed the presidency of the IOC in 1952, settling in for what would be an eventful term of office. Brundage, a founding member of the American Olympic Association, was a fierce proponent of the notion of "pure amateurism" in the Olympic movement, and was relentless in his campaign to remove politics from the Games.

MEET THE
NEW BOSS.

A former athlete, Brundage had finished sixth in the 1912 decathlon in Stockholm – which means that he was a personal competitor of Jim Thorpe's in that event.

Thorpe, who would eventually be stripped of his Stockholm medals for having accepted paltry sums as a member of a semipro baseball team in the U.S., would eventually have his medals reinstated … **but not while Brundage was president. Ever wonder why?**

Historians would later confirm that it was Brundage himself who, in 1912, after losing to Thorpe, alerted officials to Thorpe's relationship with the semipro team ... and thus destroyed his Olympic career and reputation.

56

CRITICS HAVE POINTED TO AN APPARENT DOUBLE STANDARD DURING BRUNDAGE'S PRESIDENCY ... A **DARK SIDE** TO HIS LEGENDARY TENURE.

HE WAS EAGER TO **DENOUNCE** "PROFESSIONAL" ATHLETES WHO ACCEPTED CASH FOR COMPETING IN THEIR SPORT OF CHOICE ...

BUT ... HE TURNED A BLIND EYE TO **"SHAMATEUR" ATHLETES** FROM EASTERN BLOC NATIONS WITH (NOMINAL) DAY JOBS.

SO ...HUNDREDS OF OLYMPIC ATHLETES WERE CONSIDERED AMATEURS ... EVEN THOUGH THEIR GOVERNMENTS **BLATANTLY SUBSIDIZED** THEIR TRAINING REGIMENS AND LIFESTYLES.

YOU GOT A PROBLEM WITH THAT?

1956: Cold War, Cold Slopes

HEY ... WHAT'S THE FRENCH-CANADIAN WORD FOR *UPSET?*

It was a close affair, Austria's 1956 victory in the pairs figure skating competition. The strong favorites were Canadians Frances Dafoe and Norris Bowden, the two-time world champions. During a crucial sequence in their program, however, Dafoe and Bowden muffed a lift and, in recovering, lost precious time. As a result, they finished their routine after their music had concluded. That left the door open for Austrians **Elisabeth "Sissy" Schwarz** and **Kurt Oppelt**, whose graceful, poised routines had featured no such gaffe.

Judges opted, by a 6-3 margin, for the Austrians. Their narrow victory marked one of the notable upsets in the history of the Winter Games.

For the first time in Olympic history – but definitely not the last – the team from the Soviet Union led in the total medal count, with sixteen. Securing the spot as the top-performing Winter Olympics squad in the free world, Austria placed second, with eleven total medals.

Austria picks up speed.

WHO SAYS WE'RE ONLY FAMOUS FOR *THE SOUND OF MUSIC?*

Downhill skier Toni Sailer is the first athlete to win all three Olympic Alpine competitions.

Snow Tube

THESE WERE THE FIRST WINTER OLYMPICS TO BE *TELEVISED.*

BOLIVIA AND *IRAN* COMPETED AT THE WINTER OLYMPICS FOR THE FIRST TIME. NEITHER COUNTRY WON MEDALS.

THERE WAS AN EMBARRASSING SHORTAGE OF *SNOW* IN NORTHERN ITALY THIS YEAR.

Golden moments....

The Americans picked up five of the six available medals in the individual figure skating competitions, ceding only a bronze to Austria…Italy took the two-man bobsled competition; Switzerland came in first in the four-man contest …. Americans Hayes Alan Jenkins and Tenley Albright took gold in the men's and ladie's figure skating events, respetively … The Soviet Union placed first in the ice hockey tournament, with the U.S. taking the silver and the Canadians, formerly the owners of this event, settling for bronze …Hallgeir Brendan of Norway took the 15-kilometer Nordic skiing gold … Yevgeniy Grishin of the Soviet Union took two gold medals in speed skating.

1956: Thunder Down Under

THEY'RE ALL FOR MY MOM.

Swimmer Dawn Fraser, the central figure in one of the Olympics' most inspiring human interest stories, took her first gold medal in Melbourne, winning the ladies' 100 meters freestyle competition. But the greatest drama of her Olympic career was yet to unfold

She would win gold again in 1960 in Rome in the same event ... and then receive a devastating blow as she was preparing for the 1964 games in Tokyo: she would be involved a horrific auto accident, just months before the Games were to begin, that would traumatize her and take the life of her beloved mother. Eight years after her initial triumph in Australia, she would regroup, refocus, and re-engage – and, in memory of her mother, become the first swimmer to win Olympic gold in the same event three straight times.

Thrill of victory, agony of ... exuberance? Soviet rower Vyacheslav Ivanov was so excited at his first place finished that he literally jumped for joy. When he came down, he realized he had dropped his medal into the lake. He dove for the gold after having just rowed for it ... but couldn't locate the medal.

The Summer Games ... of November?

THAT'S WHEN IT'S SUMMER *HERE.* DEAL WITH IT.

Owing to Australia's presence in the Southern Hemisphere, where seasonal patterns play out in a mirror image of those in the Northern Hemisphere, the Games were held in November of 1956. The 2000 Sydney Games will chose a mid-September start.

The Olympics, Australian Style

There were logistical hurdles to address in Melbourne:

EQUESTRIAN EVENTS WERE HELD, NOT IN AUSTRALIA, BUT IN **SWEDEN**, MONTHS BEFORE THE REST OF THE COMPETITIONS.

THE REASON? STRICT AUSSIE **QUARANTINE LAWS** THAT FORBID THE TRANSPORT OF HORSES TO MELBOURNE.

MELBOURNE
22 NOV–3 DEC 1956

THIS MARKED THE FIRST TIME EVENTS FROM THE SAME OLYMPICS WERE HELD IN MORE THAN ONE COUNTRY.

East German and West German teams combine forces under the flag of the "Unified Team of Germany," an arrangement that will hold up until the Summer Games of 1968, when the two teams once again compete under separate flags. Between these Olympics and those held in Tokyo in 1964, victorious German athletes hear Beethoven's "Ode to Joy" instead of a national anthem.

FRANKLY, I THINK YOU GUYS ARE BEING A LITTLE **PARANOID.**

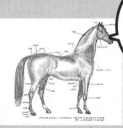

Golden moments....

Despite a number of nations boycotting for various political reasons, the Games established a trans-national rapport that served as a welcome respite from the global tensions of 1956, and became known as the "Friendly Games."This was thanks in part to the choice of athletes to parade together, rather than with their national teams, during the closing ceremonies … Soviet long-distance runner Vladimir Kuts won gold medals in the 5,000 meter and 10,000 meter events … Australian Betty Cuthbert snagged three gold medals in running events, as did American Bobby Joe Morrow … Laszlo Papp of Hungary successfully defended the light-middleweight boxing gold that he had won win 1952 in Helsinki … Egil Danielsen set a world record in the javelin throw and won the gold for Norway … A tense water-polo match rife with political implications pitted the Russians against the Hungarians; when a Hungarian had to leave because of a cut above his eye, the game became known as the "Blood in the Water Match." The game was called and awarded to Hungary, which led at the time, 4-0, and went on to win the gold medal … The Soviet Union led the final medal count, with 37 golds and 98 total medals.

1960: California Dreams

SPUTNIK'S GOT *NOTHIN'* ON ME!

Siberian schoolteacher Lydia

Skoblikova (right) snagged two gold medals in the speed skating competition. She would win four more individual medals in Innsbruck four years later. Skoblikova's was one of a number of Soviet Olympic achievements at Squaw Valley that suggested a different level of training accessible to "amateurs" within the Communist world than was available to "amateurs" outside of it. Translation: The governments of the U.S. or Great Britain weren't about to build special government-sponsored training centers for, say, schoolteachers who happened to be talented speed skaters, and then allow them to put their day jobs on hold when it was time to train.

The questions about what did and did not constitute "amateurism" grew more pointed as the years passed. Skoblikova may have been a schoolteacher, but this was no "academic" issue. She was part of a global chess game between the superpowers. For better or for worse, the Olympics were now one of the stages where high-profile geopolitical rivalries played themselves out.

Squaw Valley officials, short on cash, opted not to build a bobsled track, making these the only Winter Games at which the event was not contested.

This whole room had less computing power than your laptop.

WOW! WHO NEEDS *PUNCH CARDS* ANYMORE?

An IBM 305 RAMAC – a very early model computer – helped scorekeepers keep track of the data. This was the first time electronic computing equipment was used to tabulate Olympic results.

What a Show!

There was high drama at the 1960 Squaw Valley Olympics:

U.S. MOVIEMAKER AND ENTERTAINMENT MOGUL *WALT DISNEY* WAS NAMED HEAD OF PAGEANTRY.

IN A *MAJOR UPSET,* THE U.S. ICE HOCKEY TEAM TOOK THE GOLD, OVERCOMING SQUADS FROM THE U.S.S.R. AND CZECHOSLOVAKIA.

YIKES! THE TITLE GAME STARTED AT *EIGHT IN THE MORNING!*

Golden moments....

Soviet speed skater Yevgeny Grishin took the 500 meter event, and tied with Roald Aas of Norway for first place in the 1500 meter contest ... France's Jean Vuarnet won the men's downhill skiing medal ... Sweden's Klas Lestander won the first official Olympic biathlon competition ... Americans David Jenkins and Carol Heiss took the individual figure skating honors, which Canadians Barbara Wagner and Robert Paul won the pairs competition ...The Soviets easily lead the field in total medals, amassing 21 in all, seven of which were gold. The German squad captured a total of four gold medals, and the Americans three.

1960: Roman Holiday

NO COMMENT!

The phrase "too close to call" took on new meaning in Rome in 1960, as the outcome of the 100-meter freestyle race swung back and forth like a pendulum. An electronic timing system appeared to show that Lance Larson of the US had defeated Australian John Devitt by a tenth of a second, but officials declared that the race required closer review. In one of history's great examples of bureaucracy run amok, two separate panels of judges were established to determine the recipients of the two medals. Believe it or not, the first panel of judges was in charge of determining who came in first; the second, entirely separate panel was in charge of determining who came in second. You can't see *that* arrangement backfiring, can you?

Backfire it did. Both panels named Larson. The judges now faced that critical question that generally accompanies fiascoes made worse by committees: "How the heck do we get out of this?" Rather than give the American swimmer silver *and* gold medals – which, let's face it, would have been a little weird — the whole decision-making process was lobbed, like a hot potato, to a single judge. For reasons no one could seem to make out, the chief judge declared Devitt the winner, despite the evidence of the clock. The Americans protested, but to no avail.

Field shooter Vilho Ylonen of Finland scored a bull's-eye, but dropped out of medal contention as a result. He was, alas, shooting at the wrong target.

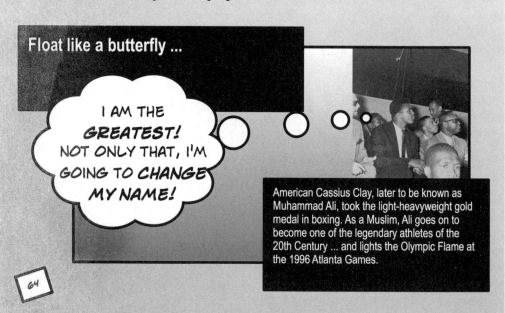

Float like a butterfly ...

I AM THE *GREATEST!* NOT ONLY THAT, I'M GOING TO *CHANGE MY NAME!*

American Cassius Clay, later to be known as Muhammad Ali, took the light-heavyweight gold medal in boxing. As a Muslim, Ali goes on to become one of the legendary athletes of the 20th Century ... and lights the Olympic Flame at the 1996 Atlanta Games.

Never Say Never

AMERICAN SWIMMER JEFF FARRELL HAD AN EMERGENCY *APPENDECTOMY* SIX DAYS BEFORE THE US OLYMPIC TEAM'S TRIALS ... HE ENDED UP WINNING THREE GOLD MEDALS IN ROME!

AMERICAN WILMA RUDOLPH, A *POLIO SURVIVOR*, WON THREE MEDALS AND EMERGED AS ONE OF THE GREAT AMERICAN CHAMPIONS.

COMING THROUGH!

UNDERRATED NEW ZEALANDERS MURRAY HALBERG (5000 METERS) AND PETER SNELL (800 METERS) POSTED GOLD-MEDAL PERFORMANCES WITHIN HOURS OF EACH OTHER.

Golden moments....

Female gymnasts from the Soviet Union very nearly post a shutout. They win fifteen of a possible sixteen total medals in their various events ... Local favorite Livio Berruti takes the 200-meter gold for Italy ....Hungarian fencer Aladar Gerevich helped his team to win the gold medal in the team sabre competition; it was the sixth straight time he had helped Hungary to secure a first-place finish in that event. (The first was back in 1932!) ... Abebe Bikila of Ethiopia won the marathon. He was barefoot at the time ... American Rafer Johnson overcame C.K. Yang in a memorable decathlon competition ... Danish cyclist Knud Enemark, who had taken amphetamines illegally, collapsed while racing, fractured his skull, and was rushed to the hospital, where he died ... The Soviets once again lead the total medal count, with 103; the Americans come in second, with 71, and host nation Italy comes in third, with 36.

WE'RE THE *FAB TWO!*

Oleg and Ludmilla Protopopov

pushed back a challenge from their German rivals Marika Kilus and Hans Jurgen Baumler, took the gold in pairs figure skating, and established a Soviet presence in the sport that would dominate many Winter Olympics to come.

The Protopopovs' combination of technical and aesthetic mastery, and their insistence on building innovative new elements into their routines, redefined figure skating. They always gave a feel of classicism to the proceedings. Their blend of innovation, classic grace, and perfectionism won over both the judges and the crowds in Innsbruck. It would endure as a legacy even after the pair eventually yielded the stage to skaters with younger legs, flashier outfits, and more demanding moves. They remain legends in the history of the sport ... and of the Olympics.

The pair would continue to put their own distinctive, effortless spin on figure skating during most of the decade of the 1960s – and successfully defend their gold medal in Grenoble in 1968.

What do you do when you're hosting the Winter Olympics ... and fate and the elements conspire to deprive you of some of the winter weather you need? You call the Austrian army, that's what you do. Troops are pressed into service to transport ice and snow from the mountains down to the Olympic venues during the Innsbruck Olympics.

Sorry, South Africa ...

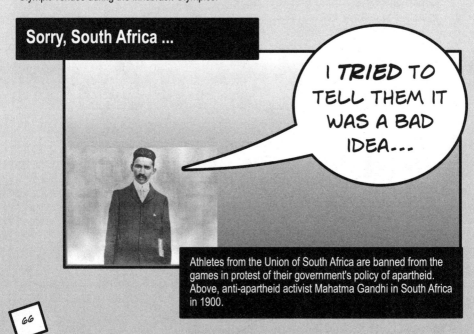

I *TRIED* TO TELL THEM IT WAS A BAD IDEA...

Athletes from the Union of South Africa are banned from the games in protest of their government's policy of apartheid. Above, anti-apartheid activist Mahatma Gandhi in South Africa in 1900.

AUSTRALIAN DOWNHILL SKIER ROSS MILNE CRASHED INTO A *TREE* DURING TRAINING AND DIED SHORTLY BEFORE THESE OLYMPICS.

THE *ENTIRE US FIGURE SKATING TEAM* HAD PERISHED IN A PLANE CRASH THREE YEARS EARLIER, SENDING THE U.S. PROGRAM INTO A PROLONGED REBUILDING PERIOD AND LEAVING THE REST OF THE GLOBAL SKATING COMMUNITY STUNNED.

TWO WEEKS BEFORE THE GAMES OPENED, ANOTHER CRASH TOOK THE LIFE OF A MEMBER OF THE *BRITISH LUGE TEAM*.

Golden moments....

Manfred Schnelldorfer, skating for a unified German team, won the top men's figure skating honors ... Sjoukje Dijkstra of the Netherlands took the ladies' gold in figure skating ... Lidia Skoblikova continued her dominance of the speed skating events, winning every event in which she competed ... Austria's Egon Zimmermann skied to victory in the men's downhill competition ... The Canadian team won gold in the four-man bobsled .... The luge made its official debut in these Olympics. Thomas Kohler of the unified German team took the medal in the men's competition ... Italian bobsled legend Eugenio Monti earned an enduring reputation for good sportsmanship. Having completed his team's run, he lent the British team a bolt that allowed them to repair their sled. Britain won the gold ... Speed skater Knut Johannesen of Norway took the men's 5,000-meter race ... The Soviets continued their winning ways, taking eleven gold medals and twenty-five medals overall.

1964: Tokyo's Turnaround

RAIN ... I DON'T MIND ...

Wet, windy weather in Tokyo didn't hold back 22-year-old Welsh long-jumper Lynn Davies. Maybe that was a result of his years of training in the persistently wet-and-windy United Kingdom, or maybe it was a burst of youthful exuberance and a desire to excel on the world athletic stage. Whatever it was, Davies leaped a staggering 8.07 meters to overcome the strong favorite, defending Olympic champion and world record holder Ralph Boston. Davies's extraordinary leap in soggy conditions was more than enough to surpass the American, and to secure the top spot on the winner's podium for Davies and Great Britain.

Davies, who ended up jumping in three Olympics, earned the nickname "Lynn the Leap" for his performance in Tokyo.

The Japanese spent approximately $3 billion to prepare for the Tokyo Games, resurrecting a city that had been ravaged by World War II and by earthquakes. These Olympics provided the Japanese people with a major morale boost, and significantly improved Japan's image abroad.

From the flames of devastation ... a torch for peace.

Yoshnori Sakai, representing the hope for future life on the planet, lit the Olympic Flame. Sakai had been born in Hitoshima (above) on August 6, 1945, the day the U.S. dropped an atomic bomb on the city.

First Time for Everything

Tokyo had more than its share of milestones in 1964:

THESE WERE THE FIRST OLYMPIC GAMES TO BE HELD IN *ASIA*.

TOKYO 1964

AMERICAN *BILLY MILLS* SHOCKED THE WORLD BY WINNING THE 10,000-METER RACE, A CONTEST WHERE NO AMERICAN HAD EVER PREVAILED.

SOMETIMES YOU EVEN SURPRISE *YOURSELF*.

JUDO MADE ITS OFFICIAL DEBUT. JAPAN WON THREE GOLDS.

SOVIET GYMNAST *LARISSA LATYNINA* CAME AWAY FROM TOKYO WITH QUITE A HAUL: TWO GOLD MEDALS, TWO SILVER, AND TWO BRONZE. THAT BROUGHT HER TOTAL FOR HER OLYMPIC CAREER TO A STAGGERING *EIGHTEEN*.

Golden moments....

The Japanese women's volleyball squad won the gold, as well as the adulation of millions of Japanese fans watching the final on live TV ... Wrestler Osamu Watanabe won the gold in freestyle wrestling for Japan and retired from Olympic competition undefeated ... Dawn Fraser won another gold in the 100-meter freestyle, her third ... American swimmer Don Schollander won four gold medals ... Having run the marathon barefoot in 1960, Abebe Bikila must have been looking for another unlikely, highly newsworthy way to run twenty-six miles without stopping. How about running the grueling race just six weeks after having had your appendix removed? Bikila did precisely that, and took the gold – this time with shoes on ... After having consistently come in second to the Soviets in the gold medal count, the Americans turned things around in Tokyo, securing a first-place finish with 36 first-place medals. The Soviets led in total medals, however, with ninety-six.

1968: Peggy's Spotlight

For a whole generation of figure skating enthusiasts, the so-called "modern" era of the sport began with American Peggy Fleming's gold medal in the ladies' competition in Grenoble in 1968. There were at least two big reasons for Fleming's enduring influence as the first great "ice queen" of the sport – and note that we use the term "ice queen" in the nicest possible sense!

The first reason for Fleming's impact had to do with what would today be called "advances in communications technology." These Olympics were the first to be broadcast on television in color, which meant that the sporting world beyond the physical skating rink got to see Fleming's routine with greater clarity and realism than that of any other previous female skater. Those dazzling images from Grenoble helped the United States – and much of the world – to fall in love with Peggy Fleming. A second reason Fleming stood out from previous champions had to do with the poignant "backstory" that accompanied her achievement. Seven years before these Olympic games, as an eleven-year-old, Fleming had lost her coach in a tragic plane crash in which the entire United States figure skating time had perished. Fleming wasn't on the plane, but she was left without a mentor. Her steely determination to recover from the tragedy, her victory in 1968, and her remarkable energy in the decades since, essentially reinvented American figure skating.

> GRACEFUL IN GRENOBLE!

Who was that man in black?

> IT'S ALWAYS SOMETHING...

Jean-Claude Killy (above) was ultimately declared the winner of the foggy, bitterly disputed men's slalom race. Killy's arch-rival, Karl Schranz, was given a second run down the course after telling judges that a mysterious figure in black had crossed in front of him and forced him to stop. Schranz's second time was better than Killy's, but Killy won the gold medal on appeal. Apparently, Schtanz had missed a gate before the dark figure (whoever he was) crossed in front of him.

For Some, a Bitter Winter

There was more than one controversy in France in 1968:

KILLY'S CONTESTED SLALOM RACE WITH SCHRANZ IGNITED FIERCE DEBATES BETWEEN FRENCH AND AUSTRIAN SKI FANS THAT HAVE, FOUR DECADES ON, *NEVER QUITE CONCLUDED.*

THREE EAST GERMAN WOMEN'S *LUGE* COMPETITORS WERE DISQUALIFIED FOR INAPPROPRIATELY HEATING THEIR TEAMMATES. (YES -- HEATING.)

TOO DARN COLD OUT HERE.

A RISING WOMEN'S MOVEMENT RAISES SOME AWKWARD QUESTIONS FOR THE IOC. NOT COUNTING MIXED COMPETITIONS, MEN GET TO COMPETE IN 21 EVENTS; WOMEN GET TO COMPETE IN TWELVE. *FAIR?* MAYBE NOT.

EQUAL RIGHTS!

Golden moments....

Representing the host nation, French skier Jean-Claude Killy became a national hero by winning all three alpine events ... The Soviets win another gold medal in ice hockey ... Wolfgang Schwarz of Austria took the gold in men's figure skating, while the Protopopovs successfully defended their pairs gold medal of 1964 ... Sweden's Toini Gustafsson won both of the solo cross-country events and picked up a silver medal in the team contest ... Italy's Eugenio Monti led his two-man and four-man squads to gold in the bobsled event ... Norway edged the Soviet Union in the national medal count, winning six golds and 14 medals overall.

1968: Mexico City

Protests against racial inequity

weren't exactly what IOC or American officials were hoping to see on the victory stand in 1968 in Mexico City, but it's what they got from runners Tommie Smith and John Carlos, who finished first and second, respectively, in the 200-meter dash. The pair raised their fists in a "Black Power" salute that spoke eloquently of the conflicts still unresolved in a United States still struggling with formal and informal segregation, discriminatory voting practices, and unprosecuted violence against blacks.

At least all those problems have finally been addressed in the U.S. nowadays. Wait – they *haven't*? Er … back to our story.

Smith and Carlos were immediately expelled from the Games and deported from Mexico, which appears to have been more or less what they anticipated. Political statements on the victory stand were, and apparently are, not to be tolerated during the Olympic Games. Point taken, but perhaps the two American athletes had their eyes on a different kind of victory.

TELLING IT LIKE IT *IS*.

Mexico City's high-altitude air contained about one-third less oxygen than some athletes were used to, leading to complaints from many competitors, notably those in endurance sports, that the host city selection had been a poor one. Sprinters seemed to take to the rarefied climate, however, as a number of world records were set in the sprints and in jumping events.

Vera looks away.

The crowd favorite of the 1968 games had to be Czech gymnast Vera Caslavska (left), who, after having apparently won a gold medal for her floor routine, saw judges "upgrade" the scores of her Russian rival and declare a tie. The outspoken Caslavska, whose country had recently been invaded by the Soviets, had herself been forced into hiding in the weeks before the Olympics. She turned her head away in silent protest as the Soviet national anthem played.

Riots in the Streets

There was blood on the ground in Mexico in 1968:

TEN DAYS BEFORE THE OLYMPICS, **5,000 DEMONSTRATORS** GATHERED IN A PUBLIC SQUARE OUTSIDE AN APARTMENT COMPLEX AND CHANTED SLOGANS LIKE, "WE DON'T WANT THE OLYMPIC GAMES - WE WANT A REVOLUTION!"

TANKS AND ARMORED CARS SURROUNDED THE SQUARE AT SUNSET ON OCTOBER 2, 1968 AND BEGAN **FIRING** LIVE ROUNDS INTO GROUPS THAT CONTAINED BOTH PROTESTORS AND BYSTANDERS.

YOU SAY YOU WANT A REVOLUTION ...

HUNDREDS DIED. THE IOC DECIDED TO PROCEED WITH THE GAMES DESPITE THE CARNAGE.

Golden moments....

High jumper Dick Fosbury of the U.S. (above) revolutionized his event with the "Fosbury Flop" ... American discus thrower Al Oerter snagged a fourth straight gold, and his teammate Bob Beamon set a world record in the long jump on the way to a first-place finish. Another American, Dick Fosbury (right), revolutionized the high jump using the new "Fosbury flop" jumping style ... Czech gymnast Vera Caslavska won four golds and the hearts of a global television audience ... Speaking of heart: Tanzania's John Stephen Akhwari finished the marathon dead last – on a dislocated knee ... Sweden's Hans-Grunner Liljenwall was disqualified after testing positive for alcohol usage, and is banned from the pentathlon. Liljenwall is thus the first Olympic athlete to be bounced as the result of failing a drug test ... The United States team wins both the overall medal race and the race for gold, collecting 45 and 107 medals, respectively.

1972: The Snows of Sapporo

> HEY *BOSS* ... DO I GET A PROMOTION FOR WINNING GOLD?

Norwegian policeman

Magnar Solberg was introduced to the biathlon, the sport with which his name will forever be linked, by his boss, a former Olympic cross-country skier. His ranking officer, in fact, was the one who trained him in the sport, which combines cross-country skiing with target practice.

The routine-sounding word "training" actually doesn't do justice to what Solberg had to go through to win his two gold medals in this demanding event, which combines cross-country skiing with rifle target shooting. (The first medal came his way in 1968 in Grenoble; he won the second in these Olympic Games.) "Ordeal" is probably a better description. Solberg's coach made him run long distances in the broiling heat of the summer, the better to build up strength for this winter event. In order to perfect his marksmanship, Solberg was ordered to conduct target practice on the inhabitants of a live anthill. Bad for the ants, yes, but good for an aspiring biathlete hoping to steady his aim. The hard work paid off. Solberg became the first man to win consecutive first-place finishes in the biathlon.

Canada boycotts the Sapporo games in protest of the Soviet-bloc system of training and supporting dubiously "amateur" athletes. Disputes over eligibility rules are becoming a threat to the Olympic movement itself. (See below.)

Brundage has a hissy fit.

> JUST *WAIT* TILL I'M IN CHARGE ...

IOC president Avery Brundage, himself a 1912 Olympian (left), was now, he assured the world, running the show. Dammit. In early 1972, he sent signals that he'd finally had enough, and that he was going to make examples out of Alpine skiers who had accepted money from ski equipment manufacturers in return for what could euphemistically be labeled "promotional consideration." Ultimately, though, Brundage *didn't* suspend 40 of the top downhill skiers in the world. Instead, he singled out Austrian Karl Schranz and barred him from the Sapporo Games.

Governments that made a habit of sidestepping the rules about subsidizing athletes (by, for instance, paying athletes to serve as "employees" in cushy or nonexistent jobs) still got a free pass. The entire eligibility system was, by 1972, an utterly unworkable mockery, and drastically in need of an overhaul. Brundage, however, was not the man to give it that overhaul.

Rapid Transitions

Change was in the mountain air at the Sapporo Games:

OLÉ!

FRANCISCO FERNANDEZ-OCHOA WON THE SLALOM .. AND BECAME THE FIRST SPANIARD TO WIN GOLD AT THE WINTER GAMES.

WOODEN SKIS MADE THEIR FINAL APPEARANCE ON THE FEET OF CONTENDING SKIERS IN THESE GAMES.

(AFTER 1972, EVERYONE OF NOTE SWITCHED TO HIGH-TECH SYNTHETIC SKIS.)

Golden moments....

Beatrix Schuba of Austria took the ladies' figure skating gold; Ondrej Nepela of Czekhoslovakia won top men's honors. Irina Rodnina and Aleksei Ulanov of the USSR won the pairs competition .... Japan, which up to this point had never won gold in the Winter Games, picked up first, second and third place medals in the ski jump competition ... Americans Anne Henning and Diane Hollum were standouts in the ladies' speed skating competition; Ard Schenk of the Netherlands won three gold medals in the men's speed skating competition ... Marie-Theres Nadig of Switzerland scored a huge upset with a victory in the women's downhill and giant slalom contests ... The Soviet Union led the way with eight gold medals and sixteen total medals. One of the top performers on that squad was Galina Kulokova, who won all three gold medals in the women's cross country.

1972: Terror.

Tragedy struck the Olympics when a Palestinian terrorist group, Black September, raided a poorly-secured Olympic Village and then kidnapped, held hostage, and eventually murdered eleven Israeli athletes and coaches. The group's demands that over 200 imprisoned allies in Israel and Germany be released were never met; all of the terrorists were killed in an armed assault at the Munich airport.

IOC President Avery Brundage chose to continue the Games after the massacre of the Israeli athletes, opting for a single day of mourning. The decision was controversial.

The world mourned, and the Olympic flame burned, as the Games went on.

1972: The Games Go On

In one of the bitterest sporting controversies in Olympic history, the Soviet Union took the gold medal in basketball from a United States squad that couldn't quite bring itself to believe what it saw happening on the court.

In a gold-medal game already rich with Cold War implications, the Americans took their first lead of the game with just three seconds left on the clock. A single point, and three ticks on the clock, appeared to be all that separated them from a triumph over their Soviet rivals. The clock wound down to one second left before the officials realized that the Russians had been attempting to take a time out.

What happened next defied – and continues to defy – description. Play resumed and time appeared to expire, and the American team began to celebrate. But the officials spotted a problem with the clock and ordered the teams to restart play. Then spotted another problem, and ordered another restart . Each time, the officials were attempting to rectify a previous error. To American players and fans, though, the confusion looked a great deal like a series of "second chances" for the Soviet team, the last of which resulted in a buzzer-beater that officials decreed had won the game.

Americans disagreed, and, to a man, refused the silver medal in protest. Each and every member of the team eventually stipulated in his will that no descendant is ever to lay claim to the medal commemorating the team's disputed second-place finish in 1972.

TIME OUT! NO, WAIT! TIME IN AGAIN! NO, WAIT! TIME OUT! HOLD IT! HOLD IT! THE REF SAYS WE GET A *DO-OVER!*

Mark's magic

JUST CALL ME A *POOL SHARK!*

American Mark Spitz swam his way to an unprecedented seven gold medals in Munich, one of the great individual performances of any Olympics.

Night Falls in Munich

Some things went right, but a lot went wrong in Munich in 1972 :

> AMERICAN FRANK SHORTER WON THE MARATHON, BUT NOT BEFORE AN IMPOSTER WHO WAS NOT EVEN AN OLYMPIC ATHLETE JOGGED INTO THE STADIUM IN AN EFFORT TO TAKE A *FAKE VICTORY LAP.*

> PAKISTANI FIELD HOCKEY PLAYERS, ANGRY AT REFEREES, SWARMED THE OFFICIALS' TABLE AND *DOUSED* THE PRESIDENT OF THE INTERNATIONAL HOCKEY FEDERATION WITH WATER.

> AMERICAN RUNNERS VINCENT MATTHEWS AND WAYNE COLLETT, WHO HAD WON GOLD AND SILVER IN THE 400 METERS, RESPECTIVELY, WERE *BANNED FOR LIFE* FROM THE OLYMPICS FOR JOKING CASUALLY AND PLAYING WITH THEIR MEDALS DURING THE U.S. NATIONAL ANTHEM.

> ALL KINDS OF BAD ENERGY AT THESE OLYMPICS, MAN...

Golden moments....

Petite Soviet teenager Olga Korbut takes three gold medals and ignites a media frenzy. Her emotional floor routine is a turning point in the history of women's gymnastics .... Finland's Lasse Viren won the 10,000 meter race despite a fall; he also won the 5,000 meter contest ... US runners Ray Robinson and Eddie Hayes were not given proper instructions on when to show up for their races; they were eliminated from contention in the 100 meter and 200 meter races. Soviet runner Valeri Borzov stepped through the open door and won gold in both events ... Australian teenager Shane Gould would have been the swimming story of these Olympics had it not been for the extraordinary achievements of Mark Spitz. Gould, only 15, took three gold medals, a silver, and a bronze ... The Soviet Union led the way in both the total medal count (99) and the gold medal race (50).

Part Three:
After Avery

Amateur Hour

THE TIMES THEY ARE A-CHANGIN'...

Arguments over who should and shouldn't be allowed to compete in the modern Olympic Games had been going on for decades. But the global rivalry between communist and capitalist systems had brought new urgency to the debate. Was a Russian who had spent years preparing for the Olympics at state expense really in the same category as an Englishman or an American who had no access to state support? For two decades, as head of the IOC, Avery Brundage had essentially sidestepped the problem, pretending that a constantly repeated standard for "amateurism" resolved all the issues. It didn't.

The rules were outdated. Brundage's retirement made possible a new look at the realities facing both nations and Olympic athletes.

1974...

... A YEAR BEST KNOWN FOR SMILEY FACES, REEL-TO-REEL TAPE RECORDERS, AND THE NIXON RESIGNATION, WAS ACTUALLY A **BANNER YEAR** FOR THE OLYMPIC MOVEMENT.

NO OLYMPIC SPORTING EVENTS WERE HELD THAT YEAR, BUT THE WORD **"AMATEURISM"** WAS DROPPED FROM THE OLYMPIC CHARTER.

THERE WERE NO FORMAL POLICY CHANGES CONNECTED TO THIS "EDITORIAL" CHANGE ... BUT THE SIGNAL WAS CLEAR. THE IOC, UNDER NEW MANAGEMENT, WAS ON A FAST TRACK TOWARD **REFORM** OF ITS ELIGIBILITY STANDARDS.

"FAST TRACK" BY IOC STANDARDS, THAT IS. NOTHING ELSE OF CONSEQUENCE WOULD HAPPEN ON THIS ISSUE UNTIL 1981.

IN THE MEANTIME, THERE WAS **ANOTHER PROBLEM** THAT NEEDED ADDRESSING ...

Illegal doping

OUR MOTTO: BETTER LIVING THROUGH *CHEMISTRY!*

What was up in the East German Olympic program? Something odd had been noticeable since Munich. East German athletes were starting to show up for international competitions bigger, stronger, and faster than their counterparts from other nations. Not just a little bigger, faster, and stronger. A whole lot bigger, faster, and stronger.

East Germany, a nation of only 17 million people, was emerging as an Olympic force to be reckoned with. It had more than doubled its gold medal count in the Munich Games. Were clandestine drug treatments part of the reason?

84

THE EAST GERMANS DENIED IT.

EVEN AS THEY DID SO, HOWEVER, ATHLETES FROM OTHER NATIONS COULDN'T HELP NOTICING THE *EVER-MORE-GARGANTUAN* SIZE, STRENGTH, AND SPEED OF EAST GERMAN COMPETITORS.

RUMORS FLEW. WAS THE EAST GERMAN REGIME REALLY FINDING WAYS TO DOPE ATHLETES THAT WOULD ESCAPE THE NOTICE OF OLYMPIC DRUG TESTS?

THE ANSWERS WOULD EVENTUALLY EMERGE ... AND WHEN THEY DID, THEY WOULD *NOT BE PRETTY.*

IN THE MEANTIME, OTHER COUNTRIES FELL UNDER SUSPICION AS WELL.

1976: Back to Innsbruck

WHAT GOES DOWN, *FAST*, MUST WIN GOLD...

Denver, Colorado was supposed to be the site of this year's Games, but the residents of that fair city balked when it came time to approve funding for the (frequently unprofitable) honor of hosting the Winter Olympics. Innsbruck, Austria, which hosted the 1964 games, steps up to the demanding, high-profile, and financially dubious task, approving a second round of Winter Games against the backdrop of some magnificent mountain ranges.

Magnificent – and dangerous. Skiier **Franz Klammer,** competing for the host nation, faces a particularly daunting set of conditions in the downhill skiing competition, but overcomes the icy challenges presented by the familiar course to win the gold medal by a third of a second. Klammer's wild ride down the mountain course, seemingly on the edge of disaster, then regaining his balance, was one of the highlights of the Games.

Ice dancing made its debut as an official Olympic sport.

Something odd ...

WHAT'S UP WITH THE EAST GERMANS?

DON'T ASK ...

The East Germans outpace historic Winter Olympic powerhouses Norway, the United States, and Austria in the overall medal count. Rumors of doping intensify.

The Sixteen-Year Streak

A long and winding road started in 1976 in Innsbruck:

RAISA SMETANINA OF THE U.S.S.R. BEGAN A REMARKABLE STREAK IN *WOMEN'S CROSS COUNTRY.*

SHE WOULD WIN A MEDAL OF SOME KIND IN THIS EVENT IN *EVERY WINTER OLYMPICS* BETWEEN 1976 AND 1992!

HER FINAL MEDAL, IN 1992, CAME JUST WEEKS BEFORE HER *40TH BIRTHDAY!*

CALL ME THE *IRON WOMAN.*

Golden moments....

The Soviet team won the ice hockey gold for the fourth consecutive Winter Olympics ... American Dorothy Hamill took the gold in women's figure skating; shortly thereafter her pert haircut quickly launched a pre-emptive assault on U.S. popular culture. Can you name the winner of the men's skating gold? Neither can anyone else. Well, the English probably can. It was John Curry, of Great Britain ... The East Germans began a long streak of victories in the four-man bobsled ... Jan Egil Storhult of Norway took the 1500-meter speed skating gold in the men's competition; Galina Stepanskaya won the corresponding women's race for the Soviet Union ... The Russians surpassed the East Germans in the overall medal count, 27-19.

1976: Going for Broke

"I did not even look at the scoreboard when my routine was done in 1976," Romanian gymnast Nadia Comaneci would recall in an interview decades after her historic triumph in women's gymnastics at the Montreal Olympics. "My teammates started pointing because there was an uproar." The uproar was the result of a perfect ten – an unprecedented declaration from the judges that the diminutive Comaneci had performed at a level that could not possibly be surpassed. Watching the tape of her performance, it's hard to disagree – but Comaneci herself was, at the time, among those who considered the point debatable, "I did not think it was all that perfect," she opined in later years. "I thought it was pretty good, but athletes don't think about history when they are making history. They think about what they're doing, and that's how it gets done. "

HAPPINESS IS A *TEN!*

Staggering deficits afflict the Montreal Games. When the dust settles, organizers estimate that these Olympics have lost over two billion Canadian dollars. (That's "billion," with a "B".) The news has a chilling effect on future games, as fewer aspiring host cities vie for the right to go broke.

"Uh ... why do you want to check my foil?"

THINK OF IT AS A *LIGHT SABER!*

Soviet fencer boris Onyschenko draws the attention of officials when he scores points without touching his opponent. An examination of his foil leads to the discovery that he has wired it in a way that allows him to score points at will by pressing a button.

88

BOXER **CLARENCE HILL** OF BERMUDA (POPULATION 50,000) WON A BRONZE MEDAL IN THE SUPER-HEAVYWEIGHT DIVISION, THEREBY EARNING A UNIQUE DISTINCTION. NO ATHLETE FROM A LESS POPULOUS NATION HAD EVER CAPTURED AN OLYMPIC MEDAL.

JAPANESE GYMNAST **SHUN FUJIMOTO** BROKE HIS LEG DURING A FLOOR ROUTINE, BUT DIDN'T TELL ANYONE. HE EVENTUALLY DISLOCATED HIS KNEE WHILE DISMOUNTING FROM A RINGS EXERCISE AND HAD TO BOW OUT OF THE COMPETITION.

WHAT ABOUT ME? I WAS IN THE WORST DISCO FILM EVER MADE, **CAN'T STOP THE MUSIC!**

HUNGARY'S **MIKLOS NEMETH** CAME IN FIRST IN THE JAVELIN THROW; TWENTY-EIGHT YEARS EARLIER, HIS FATHER, IMRE NEMETH, HAD WON THE GOLD MEDAL IN THE HAMMER THROW.

Golden moments....

Bruce Jenner (above) won the decathlon. The Hollywood career that followed, however, was less inspiring ... African nations boycotted the games to protest the New Zealand rugby team's choice to compete in apartheid South Africa before the Olympics .... Diuedone Lamothe of Haiti runs the heat for 5000 meter race at a surrealistically poor pace, coming in last and posting the worst time in Olympic history. Some people wonder why he didn't drop out. Apparently, he couldn't. Haitian dictator Baby Doc Duvalier had reportedly promised to execute him if he didn't cross the finish line ... American boxers Ray Leonard, Leon Spinks, and Michael Spinks won gold ... Great Britain wins the modern pentathlon ... The Soviet Union easily amasses more gold medals, and more total medals, than any other nation. East Germany comes in second.

1980: New York State of Mind

IT'S THE *NEW ICE AGE!*

Think of your kitchen. Now think of the shiny metal appliance into which you place bread when you want to lightly singe the outer surface of the bread before buttering it and eating. Now think of the bread that has undergone this light-singing process. What's the word for that kind of lightly cooked bread again? Oh, yes. Toast.

Toast is what the U.S. hockey team was expected by all the experts to resemble at the conclusion of its qualifying contest with the Soviet Union. After all, a gaggle of raw, inexperienced college kids couldn't really expect to dominate a squad of hard-checking, government-subsidized hockey behemoths, could they? Not only did they expect such a thing – they did it, 4-3, then went on to beat Finland for the gold medal, 4-2. The part every American of a certain age remembers today is not the score, but U.S. broadcaster Al Michaels practically having a coronary as the final seconds ticked down. ("Do you believe in miracles? YESSSS!") The U.S. team's odyssey was dubbed the "Miracle on Ice," and eventually turned into an above-average sports movie, *Miracle*.

Lake Placid had. as students of Olympic history will no doubt recall, also hosted the Winter Olympics back in 1932. The opening ceremonies featured remembrances of those Depression-era Games.

Let it snow. And if it doesn't...

BRR ...

Artificial snow machines supplemented the occasionally meager snow cover in Lake Placid in 1980, the first time such machinery was used at a Winter Olympics.

90

The winner is ... who?

Unlikely Lichtenstein mounted another major upset in Lake Placid:

HANNI WENZEL, OF TINY LICHTENSTEIN (WHICH BOASTED ALL OF 25,000 CITIZENS), WON BOTH THE SLALOM AND GIANT SLALOM RACES.

BE HONEST: DID YOU EVEN KNOW THERE **WAS** A LICHTENSTEIN?

SHE ALSO WON THE SILVER IN THE **DOWNHILL.**

HER **THREE-FOR-THREE** PERFORMANCE WAS ONE OF THE GREAT OLYMPIC UPSETS. IT GAVE HOPE TO LITTLE NATIONS EVERYWHERE ... BUT LICHTENSTEIN'S DAYS AS AN OLYMPIC POWERHOUSE HAVE, SO FAR, BEEN LIMITED TO HANNI AND 1980.

Golden moments....

Soviet figure skater Irina Rodnina won an unprecedented third gold medal in the pairs competition. The first had come in 1972 with partner Aleksey Ulanov; her partner in 1976 and 1980 was Alekseay Ulanov ... American Eric Heiden cops the gold in five out of five speed skating competitions. His five gold medals make up five-sixth of the total U.S.golds ... Robin Cousins of Great Britain wins the men's figure skating competition; Anett Poetzch takes the women's title ... Jouko Tormanen of Finland took the gold in the large hill ski jumping event ... Toni Innauer of Austria took the medal in ski jumping on the normal hill... East Germany won more total medals than the Soviet squad.

America hits the brakes

To protest the Soviet invasion of Afghanistan, the U.S. led a boycott of the Olympic Games scheduled for Moscow in 1980.

Athletes who might have been thinking about going to go to Moscow on their own, American president Jimmy Carter decreed, should think again. Their passports would be revoked.

Cold War politics carried the day ... and American athletes weren't the only ones who paid the price.

THE BOYCOTT CAUGHT ON.

UNDER INTENSE U.S. PRESSURE, LOTS OF COUNTRIES AGREED TO **SKIP** THE 1980 OLYMPICS.

CRITICS ACCUSED CARTER OF **GRANDSTANDING** FOR POLITICAL REASONS. (HE WAS RUNNING FOR RE-ELECTION AT THE TIME.)

POSTSCRIPT: WHAT **GOES AROUND COMES AROUND** ... THIS U.S. BOYCOTT LAID THE GROUNDWORK FOR THE RUSSIAN "REVENGE BOYCOTT" OF 1984.

AND I THOUGHT THE ANCIENT **SPARTANS** AND **ATHENIANS** HAD A COMMUNICATION PROBLEM....

1980: Less Is More

Boycott? What boycott? Cuban boxer **Teofilo Stevenson**, winner of gold medals in the super-heavyweight division in 1972 and 1976, had no time to discuss geopolitical issues during the Moscow Games of 1980.

He was too busy planning his defense of his Olympic title … a plan that no boxer before him had ever been able to execute. Stevenson's aim was to become the first fighter in Olympic history to win a gold medal in the same weight class three times in a row.

He did it, and he solidified his status as a Cuban national hero in the process. Stevenson, who easily ranked as one of the greatest boxers in Olympic history, refused to enter the ranks of the pros after his unprecedented Olympic triumph in Moscow.

BOYCOTT *THIS.*

No, your eyes did not deceive you. Identical twins Bernd and Jorg Landvoigt took the pairs rowing competition for East Germany. When the waters were still, they looked like Olympic quadruplets, but they still only got one medal apiece.

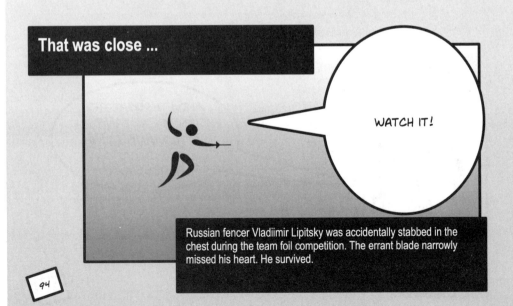

That was close ...

WATCH IT!

Russian fencer Vladiimir Lipitsky was accidentally stabbed in the chest during the team foil competition. The errant blade narrowly missed his heart. He survived.

Wish You Were Here

THE AMERICAN–LED *BOYCOTT* WAS THE MOST EFFECTIVE IN OLYMPIC HISTORY.

ONLY *EIGHTY* NATIONS COMPETED IN MOSCOW.

AS A LAST–MINUTE SOLUTION TO THE PROBLEM OF TOO FEW *FIELD HOCKEY* SQUADS, A TEAM FROM ZIMBABWE WAS INVITED, ESSENTIALLY TO FILL OUT THE EVENT.

HAPPY TO HELP OUT...

ZIMBABWE ENDED UP WINNING THE GOLD!

Golden moments....

Vladimir Salnikov (left), the "monster in the waves," took three gold medals in the swimming events for the U.S.S.R. ... Aleksander Dityatin won an unprecedented eight medals in men's gymnastics for the Soviet Untion ... Peter Baczaco of Hungary was the upset winner in the 90 kg weightlifting event ... Athletes shattered records with regularity in Moscow: 36 world records and 74 Olympic records were set ... The Soviets led the way with 80 gold medals, followed by East Germany with 47. These two nations far outstripped all other competitors: Bulgaria came in third with 8 gold medals.

Passing the Buck

IN A *GOOD* WAY, THAT IS.

That distant whirring sound people heard in 1981? It might have been Avery Brundage spinning in his grave.

The IOC finally reforms its eligibility standards, and it does so through a classic piece of bureaucratic evasion: It passes the responsibility for an important decision on to someone else. Actually, *lots* of someone elses ...

From this point on, dozens of international sports federations, not the IOC, will determine the vexing question of who gets to compete in the Olympics. The "amateurism question" is out of the IOC's hands.

SIGNS OF THE TIMES

OLYMPIC GREAT *JIM THORPE'S* MEDALS ARE REINSTATED ... *POSTHUMOUSLY.*

THE THORPE DECISION IS FAR MORE THAN IOC *SYMBOLISM.*

IT SENDS THE MESSAGE THAT HAIR-SPLITTING OVER AN ATHLETE'S AMATEUR STATUS WILL EVENTUALLY BECOME A *THING OF THE PAST.*

And as if that weren't enough change ...

The "shameless commerce" department opens for business. Taking a cue from the disastrous financial losses in Montreal, the IOC votes in 1983 to open the Olympics up to corporate sponsorship.

HEY ...

... IF YOU ALWAYS END UP NEARLY *BANKRUPTING* YOUR HOST CITY ... YOU'RE GOING TO *RUN OUT* OF HOST CITIES BEFORE TOO LONG!

1984: Sarajevo Shines

LET'S FACE THE MUSIC AND *DANCE.*

Yugoslavia's Winter Games were held in the very city – Sarajevo – where the catastrophe that was to become the First World War had, seven decades before, been ignited by a single nobleman's assassination, and where failures of diplomacy and statecraft cost humanity millions of lives. The implied message was inspiring: Even cities that gave rise to grotesque international infernos can eventually become models of peace, coexistence, and the Olympic spirit. Unfortunately, the city, the region, and the country were to disintegrate in the 1990s after the death of the dictator Tito, and the old spasms of sectarian hatred and violence would return. At the time, though, the 1984 Olympics seemed to symbolize a civilizing, stabilizing progression of humanity that would have done even de Coubertin, the first president of the IOC, proud.

War raged again in 1991. The only pride that actually turned out to be justified in 1984 was that of the athletes, and British ice dancers **Jayne Torvill** and **Christopher Dean** had perhaps the proudest moment. Radiating confidence and ambition, they copped their second straight gold medal in the ice dancing competition, solidifying their dominance in an event that they appeared, for all the world, to have rebuilt pretty much on their own terms. One remarkable program from the British duo delivered unanimous 6.0 – that is, perfect – scores from the judges for artistic impression, proving that athletics, unlike statecraft and diplomacy, is one realm where perfection may be attained.

A major upset in the downhill skiing competition saw Bill Johnson of the United States take the gold medal, edging out favorites from Switzerland and Austria.

Strange but true ...

ARE YOU A METAPHOR FOR SECTARIAN VIOLENCE?

Contests were held in Yugoslavian newspapers to select the mascot of the 1984 Winter Games. Readers chose a rather menacing-looking wolf named Vucko.

Tito's Big Show

DIMINUTIVE AMERICAN SKATER **SCOTT HAMILTON** (BELOW) TOOK THE MEN'S GOLD.

SKIER **JURE FRANKO** EARNED YUGOSLAVIA'S FIRST-EVER MEDAL IN THE WINTER OLYMPICS WITH A SECOND-PLACE FINISH IN THE GIANT SLALOM.

FINLAND'S **MARJA-LIISA HAMALAINEN** TOOK ALL THREE GOLD MEDALS IN INDIVIDUAL CROSS-COUNTRY SKIING.

I'M DOING THIS FOR THE **LITTLE GUYS.**

Golden moments....

West Germany's Katarina Witt won the women's figure skating title, overcoming Rosalyn Sumners of the United States and Kira Ivanova of the Soviet Union ... Canadian Gaetan Boucher took two gold medals in men's speed skating ... The Soviets overcame Czechoslovakia to take the gold medal in the hockey tournament ... Norwegian Eirik Kvalfoss won a gold, a silver, and a bronze in the three biathlon events ... East Germany collected more gold medals than any other nation, while the Soviets claimed first place in the total medal count ... Troubling questions about the possible illicit doping of athletes continued.

99

The U.S.S.R. hits the brakes

IVAN SAYS "NYET"!

Supposedly because of security concerns, the U.S.S.R. led an Eastern Bloc boycott of the 1984 Summer Olympic in Los Angeles.

Everybody knew what this was really about, though: Payback.

The Soviet boycott quickly became known as the "revenge boycott." It was a clear retaliation for the U.S.-led boycott of the Moscow Games in 1980.

CLEARLY...

THE POLITICAL TIT-FOR-TAT THING IS *GETTING OUT OF HAND.*

AS IF TO COMPENSATE FOR THIS, THE IOC APPROVES THE MOST DRASTIC *SCHEDULE OVERHAUL* IN ITS HISTORY.

STARTING IN 1992, IT DECREES, THOSE STIRRING OLYMPIC MOMENTS OF *GLOBAL UNITY* WILL HAPPEN EVERY *TWO* YEARS, RATHER THAN EVERY FOUR YEARS.

WINTER AND SUMMER GAMES WILL BE *STAGGERED.*

THE NEW SCHEDULE ALSO MAKES IT EASIER TO PLAN THE GAMES.

1984: The Ka-Ching Olympics

After Montreal, some had said that it was impossible to put on a profitable Olympics. Not so. American marketing, helped by massive corporate sponsorship, transformed the business model in Los Angeles. At the same time, American *athletes* stormed the Summer Games in convincing fashion, dominating so thoroughly in the absence of Soviet-bloc athletes that they eclipsed even the U.S. triumphs of the previous contests in Los Angeles, back in 1932. Instead of flickering newsreels of icons like Babe Didrikson and Buster Crabbe, a hungry nation of host-nation fans had live-feed broadcasts of a staggering array of champions to choose from. Among the most celebrated were versatile track and field star **Carl Lewis,** competing victoriously on the same stage as his idol Jesse Owens; spunky gymnast **Mary Lou Retton,** who took the women's gymnastics gold; women's marathoner **Joan Benoit,** who finished a full minute ahead of the rest of the pack; and diver **Greg Louganis,** who whacked his head on the diving board but eventually emerged, safely, on the winner's platform in the springboard competition.

Truth be told, the US dominated (and marketed) these Olympics so relentlessly that they left the rest of the world feeling just a little queasy.

LET'S HEAR IT FOR FINISHING *IN THE MONEY!*

Despite the Russian-led boycott, 140 nations took part in the 1984 Los Angeles Games. Romania defied the Eastern-bloc ban on participating in these Games, the only Communist nation to do so.

The Ueberroth games.

WHAT'S WRONG WITH *SPONSORS?*

Peter Ueberroth, organizer of the 1984 L.A. Games, wins praise from some, and derision from others, for securing high-profile corporate sponsorships.

102

"G" is for Gold ... and Green

The 1984 L.A. Olympics used corporate sponsorhsip to relight the flame:

LOS ANGELES WAS THE *ONLY* NATION TO SUBMIT A BID FOR THE GAMES THIS YEAR.

Disney

NAYSAYERS HAD POINTED TO THE TERRORIST ATTACK OF 1972, AND TO MONTREAL'S *DISMAL FINANCIAL SHOWING* IN 1976.

BUT LOS ANGELES TURNED OUT TO BE THE MOST SECURE, FINANCIALLY SUCCESSFUL OLYMPICS YET ... TURNING A PROFIT OF OVER *$200 MILLION.*

IBM

BUT AT WHAT PRICE? AT WHAT TERRIBLE, SOUL-SUCKING PRICE?

Golden moments....

The women's marathon was run for the first time; American Joan Benoit took the gold ...Al Joyner, Evelyn Ashford, and Valerie Briscoe-Hooks win gold in track and field for the U.S. ... Great Britain's Daley Thompson wins the gold medal in the decathlon ... France triumphs in the football (soccer) tournament ... Nawal El Moutawekel of Morocco pulled a major upset when she won the women's 400 meter hurdles; after hearing the news, the King of Morocco decreed that all girls born on the day of her victory were to be named after her. No statistics are available on how many Moroccan parents complied with the King's orders ... American Mary Decker and South African Zola Budd, representing Great Britan, competed in a much-hyped 3000 meter final. Budd ran into Decker, who fell and was never again in contention. Catcalls from the huge American crowd apparently got to Budd, who finished in seventh place. Maricica Puica of Romania took the gold medal ...The U.S. easily collected more gold medals (83) and total medals (174) than any other nation.

1988: Calgary Stampede

No one had ever successfully defended an Olympic alpine event before Italy's **Alberto Tomba** came along. Why not? There were lots of theories.

Some people thought that the field of aspiring Olympians was too competitive and too well trained; some thought the demands of a mountain course on the human body in these events were simply too rigorous, and that asking someone to be in the physical condition to master them, at an interval of four years, was simply asking too much.

It all sounded a bit like the old superstition that humankind was not meant to run a mile in less than four minutes. In these Olympics, Tomba employed a barreling, late-breaking style to win both the slalom and the giant slalom in 1988. The big downhill master with the big personality would successfully defend his giant slalom medal four years later in Albertville.

NEVER TELL ME THE ODDS!

There were a total of 57 competing nations, a new high for the Winter Games. Among the unlikelier participants was earnest Jamaica, whose last-place bobsled team captured the popular imagination and inspired a Walt Disney film, *Cool Runnings*, loosely based on the team's exploits. The Jamaicans were introduced to bobsledding by Americans who saw a Jamaican pushcart derby and noticed the similarity between the two sports.

Air Edwards.

WHO SAYS YOU HAVE TO WIN GOLD TO BE AN *OLYMPIC HERO?*

Self-funded, a tad overweight, and proud of his status as Great Britain's best, and only, entrant in the ski-jumping competition, Eddie "The Eagle" Edwards competed for the joy of competition itself in Calgary. He finished last in the competition, but first in the hearts of his countrymen ... and improbable aspiring Olympians everywhere.

104

Winter Marathon

A spirit of drive and reinvention propelled the expanded Calgary Games:

THE WINTER GAMES NOW ENCOMPASSED *SIXTEEN DAYS.*

FOR THE FIRST TIME, *SMOKING* WAS PROHIBITED OUTRIGHT AT AN OLYMPIC COMPETITION.

IN ANOTHER FIRST, THE SPEED SKATING EVENTS WERE HELD *INDOORS.*

WHEE! IT'S *FASTER!*

WINTER, SUMMER, I DON'T CARE...

Golden moments....

Christa Rothenburger of East Germany (left) won the 1000 meter women's speed skating event. The following summer, she would win a silver medal in cycling, thus garnering medals in the Summer and Winter Olympics of the same year ...Yvonne Van Gennip of the Netherlands and Bonnie Blair of the U.S. also won speed skating gold ... Matti Nykanen of Finland was the top performer in the ski jumping competition ... Switzerland took the four-man bobsled event, and the Soviet team took the two-man gold ... Brian Boitano of the United States won the men's figure skating final; Katarina Witt of West Germany secured the women's gold. Soviet skaters Ekaterina Gordeeva and Sergei Grinkov came in first in the pairs competition ... The Soviet Union narrowly eclipsed East Germany in the total medal count (29-25) and in the race for most gold medals (11-9).

1988: Seoul Music

Hosting the 1988 Summer Games in Seoul, Korea was a matter of intense national pride for South Koreans – it offered proof positive of their nation's economic, cultural, and psychological rebound from the traumas of past conflicts ... including, but not limited to, the Korean War that had raged with such devastation in the early 1950s. Observers expected the potent, optimistic nationalism of the South Koreans to be on display for the first host-nation victory of the 1988 games, but they probably didn't expect the emotional outpouring that they got from wrestler **Kim Young-Nam**. When he pulled out a close 2-1 victory over Soviet wrestler Daulet Turlykhanov to become the first South Korean gold medalist of the games, Young-Nam threw decorum to the winds and started shouting and running around the ring like a madman. (The rest of the country went nuts, too.)

> I FEEL **GOOD!**
> I KNEW THAT I WOULD!

Diver Greg Louganis continued his dominance in the spring and platform diving events, and emerged as one of the truly great competitors in his sport. In later years, he would overcome a barrier of a different kind, publishing a memoir in which he acknowledged that he had the AIDS virus.

East Germany had nothing on Ben.

> FACE IT --
> I HAVE GREAT
> **PERSONAL**
> **CHEMISTRY!**

Ben Johnson of Canada finished first in the 100-meter race, but was disqualified for steroid use. Carl Lewis was awarded the gold following Johnson's disqualification.

To the Limit

KERSTIN PALM OF SWEDEN, A FENCER, BECAME THE FIRST FEMALE ATHLETE TO COMPETE IN SEVEN OLYMPICS.

SWIMMER *ANTHONY NESTY* OF SURINAME UPSET AMERICAN MATT BIONDI IN THE 100 METER BUTTERFLY.

SORRY, DUDE...

SOHN KEE-CHUNG, THE 76-YEAR-OLD WINNER OF THE 1936 OLYMPIC MARATHON, CARRIED THE OLYMPIC TORCH INTO THE STADIUM.

HE HAD BEEN FORCED TO COMPETE UNDER A JAPANESE NAME IN 1936, DUE TO JAPAN'S OCCUPATION OF KOREA.

North Korea, Ethiopia, Nicaragua, and Cuba boycotted the Games ... because North Korea was, technically, still at war with South Korea.

Golden moments....

American swimmers Matt Biondi and Janet Evans win multiple swimming gold medals, as does Kristin Otto of East Germany ... Table tennis makes its debut as an official Olympic sport; China takes two gold medals, to no one's surprise ...Two Bulgarian weightlifters fail drug tests and have their gold medals withdrawn; shortly thereafter the entire Bulgarian weightlifting team backs out of future competitions at Seoul ... The Soviet Union and East Germany, two nations that will not exist at the next Olympics, finish first and second in the overall and gold medal counts.

107

Part Four: Walls Come Down

WOW ...

The Berlin Wall that divided East and West Germany fell in 1989, and the Soviet Union disintegrated as a political entity in 1991.

As a result, the Cold War dynamic that had dominated, and often undermined, the Olympic movement was no more. The Games found themselves transitioning into an entirely new environment in the early 1990s ... and part of this change was on display with the (once-unthinkable) entrance of professional athletes into high-profile sports like basketball and figure skating.

The world was reinventing itself, and so, at long last, was the Olympic movement ...

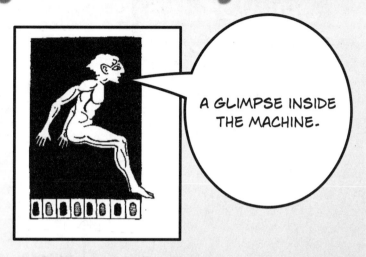

A GLIMPSE INSIDE THE MACHINE.

Renate Neufeld joined the East Berlin Sports Institute at the age of seventeen; her specialty was the 80-meter hurdles. As a condition of entry, she had to swear that she would never speak to anyone, including her parents, about East German training methods.

She set about preparing for the Olympics. Her training was rigorous. All the athletes were monitored closely, and their comings and goings were carefully recorded.

One day her trainer suggested that she take some pills to improve her performance. He told her they were vitamins.

SHE NOTICED CHANGES...

NEUFELD STARTED GETTING SEVERE CRAMPS IN HER LEGS. HER VOICE STARTED TO CHANGE. SHE WAS SOMETIMES UNABLE TO SPEAK. SHE STARTED TO GROW A MUSTACHE. *HER PERIODS STOPPED.*

SHE ANNOUNCED TO HER TRAINERS THAT SHE WOULD *NO LONGER TAKE HER "VITAMINS."*

ONE MORNING, EAST GERMAN *SECRET POLICE* APPEARED AND INTERROGATED HER ABOUT HER DECISION TO STOP TAKING THE PILLS.

SHORTLY AFTER THAT, SHE FLED THE COUNTRY.

She was one of the lucky ones!

LOTS OF ATHLETES **COULDN'T ESCAPE** THE SYSTEM, OR CHOSE NOT TO TRY.

NEUFELD'S WAS ONE OF THE FEW **FIRST-HAND** ACCOUNTS OF EAST GERMANY'S SYSTEMATIC DOPING PROGRAM TO COME OUT BEFORE THE BERLIN WALL FELL.

EAST GERMANY CONTINUED ITS DOPING PROGRAM FOR **YEARS** AFTER NEUFELD'S DEFECTION!

A living nightmare

The fall of the Berlin Wall, and the reunification of East and West Germany, led to even more disturbing revelations about the extent, and human costs, of the doping regimen that took place under the authority of the medal-hungry East German system.

East German scientists, we now know, routinely began doping future Olympic star athletes when they were as young as 13. Many of them suffered gruesome side effects in later life, including psychological problems, liver cancer, infertility, and hormone problems.

A BREAK WITH THE PAST:

FORMER WORLD RECORD HOLDER **CAROLA NITSCHKE** WAS THIRTEEN WHEN SHE BEGAN RECEIVING ORAL AND INJECTED HORMONE TREATMENTS FROM EAST GERMAN DOCTORS.

NITSCHKE FINISHED OUT OF MEDAL CONTENTION IN SEVERAL EVENTS IN THE **1976 OLYMPICS.** SHE WAS AN ALTERNATE ON THE RELAY TEAM THAT WON THE 4X100 METER MEDLEY RELAY.

AFTER THE FALL OF THE BERLIN WALL, SHE BECAME THE FIRST ATHLETE FROM THE EAST GERMAN "MEDAL MACHINE" TO REQUEST THAT HER MARKS BE **STRICKEN** FROM THE OLYMPIC RECORD BOOK.

NOBODY'S TAKEN HER UP ON IT YET.

1992: Brave New World

Germany now competed under a single flag for the first time in decades, and the man who carried that flag into the stadium was a walking, talking reminder that not everything associated with the old East German Olympic program was tainted: **Wolgang Hoppe.** Hoppe had won gold medals in both the two-man and four-man bobsled events in 1984, and had taken a silver medal in 1988 in the two-man event.

Now, he was competing for something more meaningful than gold: the chance to place an exclamation mark next to a stellar career, and remind a global audience that he had, in fact, earned his past glory. Having passed stringent drug tests, Hoppe led his team to a silver medal in Albertville in the four-man event, and the German team to a first-place finish in the overall medal count.

Hoppe thus solidified his position as one of the true greats in the history of the sport.

ONE WORD: *HONOR* ...

Algeria, Bermuda, Brazil, Honduras, Ireland, and Swaziland competed in the Winter Games for the first time. Other nations (see below) returned to the Olympic fold after long absences.

Back (out of) the U.S.S.R.

GEE, IT'S GOOD TO BE BACK IN THE OLYMPICS...

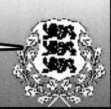

The collapse of the Soviet Union allowed teams from former Soviet republics Estonia (above) Belarus, Latvia, and Lithuania to compete as independent nations for the first time since 1936. The remaining former Soviet republics competed under the Olympic flag as part of a "Unified Team."

Comings and Goings

GERMANY ONCE AGAIN FIELDED A UNIFIED TEAM.

ANNELISE COBERGER OF NEW ZEALAND PCKED UP A SILVER IN THE WOMEN'S GIANT SLALOM.

HONDURAS AND **SWAZILAND** EACH SENT TEAMS TO THE WINTER OLYMPICS FOR THE FIRST ... AND, SO FAR, LAST ... TIMES.

HERS WAS THE FIRST WINTER OLYMPICS MEDAL FOR A NATION IN THE SOUTHERN HEMISPHERE.

YUGOSLAVIA MADE WHAT TURNED OUT TO BE ITS FINAL APPEARANCE IN THE OLYMPIC GAMES.

Golden moments....

Norwegian skier Bjorn Daehlie led his country's assault on the cross-country skiing events, winning three of the six available gold medals for men. His teammate Vegard Ulvang secured the gold medals in the other races, completing Norway's sweep ... Sixteen-year-old Finnish ski jumper Toni Nieminen won gold ... Austrian Petra Kronberger shone in the women's alpine competition, winning two gold medals ... Kristi Yamaguchi of the United States and Midori Ito of Japan finished one-two in the women's figure skating competition; Victor Petrenko of the Unified Team took gold on the men's side, followed by American Paul Wylie, who won the silver. The pairs event went to Natalia Mishkutenok and Artur Dimitriev of the Unified Team ... Germany's Gunda Niemann and America's Bonnie Blair dominated the women's speed skating events ... The newly reunified German team took the most gold medals and the most overall medals.

1992: Spanish Gold

FOR MOTHER *AFRICA!*

The women's 10,000 meter finals at the 1992 Games was not only a great battle of gifted athletes – it featured a truly inspiring finish. A strong field of European competitors was rounded out by two Africans, **Derarta Tulu** of Ethiopia and **Elana Meyer** of South Africa. They were the only two Africans in the running … and each woman ran the race of her life. On this day, the two waged one of the great races of the Barcelona Olympics. Tulu crossed the finish line first, and Meyer came in second.

One of the most memorable moments of the Olympics then followed, as the black Tulu and the white Mayer ran their victory lap together, celebrating, in a single lap, two kinds of victory: Their personal achievements on the track ... and the end of the apartheid era in South Africa.

Rifleman Rhyohei Kobe of Japan made a memorable vow in training for these Olympics, swearing to his comrades-in-arms that he will give up not only alcohol, but also singing karaoke, in pursuit of an Olympic medal. He wins a bronze.

This is synchronicity?

I'M NOT COMING UP UNTIL YOU GIVE ME THE *RIGHT SCORE.*

American Kristen Babb-Sprague wins the gold medal in synchronized swimming after a judge mistakenly enters a low score for her opponent, Sylvie Frechette of Canada, and is not allowed to correct the error after the number is flashed on the scoreboard. A little over a year later, the International Swimming Federation decides that both women deserve gold medals.

Barcelona'92

SPANISH ARCHER ANTONIO REBOLLO IGNITED THE OLYMPIC FLAME IN *DRAMATIC* FASHION.

FROM AN IMPOSING DISTANCE, HE FIRED A *FLAMING ARROW* OVER THE MASSIVE OLYMPIC CAULDRON, WHICH INSTANTLY BURST INTO *BRIGHT, HUGE FLAMES.*

GLAD I DIDN'T *MISS!*

Golden moments....

The American women's 4 x 100 relay team, which included legendary sprinter Evelyn Ashford, won gold ... Belarus's Vitaly Scherbo had a day to remember in men's gymnastics – winning four gold medals in a single day. He would end up winning a total of six golds, five of them in individual contests ... Tatiana Gutsu of the Unified Team won the women's all-around competition, narrowly eclipsing American Shannon Miller .... Swimmers Yevgeny Sadovyi and Alexandor Popov each won two individual swimming golds for the Unified Team ... For the first time, baseball was an official Olympic sport. Cuba took the gold medal ... Hungary's Krisztina Egerszegi won three gold medals in swimming .... The defending men's volleyball champions, the United States, lose a bitterly contested match with Japan, and shave their heads as a form of protest ... At the (athletically speaking) advanced age of 32, Great Britan's Linford Christie won the 100 meter dash ... The Unified Team (representing athletes from the former Soviet system) led the way in total medals and gold medals. The United States finished second and Germany third.

1994: Lillehammer

TONYA *WHO?*

A lot of bizarre things have happened to athletes in the run-up to the Olympics, but it's a pretty safe bet that the attack on American figure skater **Nancy Kerrigan** ranks as one of the Games' most surrealistic examples of rivalry run amok. During a practice session at the U.S. Figure Skating Championships, a thug struck Kerrigan on the knee with a metal baton, injuring her. The thug, it turned out, was in the employ of two men with ties to a rival skater, Tonya Harding, who went on to win a spot on the U.S. Olympic team with a first-place finish at the U.S. Championships. A media frenzy descended upon both skaters. Harding admitted to assisting in the cover-up of the attack, but insisted that she had played no part in planning it. Attempts to remove Harding from the U.S. Olympic Team hit a roadblock when Harding threatened to sue.

Kerrigan recovered from her injuries, and the two skaters actually competed against each other in the Lillehammer finals before a massive global television audience. Kerrigan won the silver; Harding finished eighth, reached a plea bargain, and was eventually banned for life from competitive skating.

Oh, yeah ... there was someone else skating in Lillehammer. Ukrainian teenager Oksana Baiul (right) skated a brilliant program and won the gold, narrowly overcoming Kerrigan.

EVER FEEL LIKE YOU'RE *EEING OVERSHADOWED?*

Give peace a chance.

OUR MESSAGE IS STRONGER THAN EVER: PLEASE STOP THE FIGHTING. STOP THE KILLING. *DROP YOUR GUNS.*

Juan Antonio Samaranch, president of the IOC, took note of the conflict in the former Yugoslavia in his closing address for these Games, and appealed to the spirit of peace that had sustained the 1984 games in Sarajevo.

Bull's Eye in Barcelona

A stunning visual moment launched the 1992 Summer Games:

I've Got a Feeling We're Not in Oslo

The Olympics returned to Norway, but a lot had changed since 1952 :

> THE CBS TELEVISION NETWORK DICTATED THE REPOSITIONING OF THE SKI JUMPING HILLS, SO AS TO OBTAIN *BETTER CAMERA ANGLES.*

> I WAS EVENTUALLY RECOVERED.

> ON THE FIRST DAY OF THE OLYMPICS, THIEVES TOOK ADVANTAGE OF A DISTRACTED NORWAY AND STOLE THE EDVARD MUNCH PAINTING *THE SCREAM* FROM OSLO'S NATIONAL MUSEUM.

> AT *LAST!*

> THIS WAS THE FIRST WINTER OLYMPICS *NOT* TO BE HELD IN THE SAME YEAR AS A SUMMER OLYMPICS.

Golden moments....

Having encountered obstacle after obstacle since 1988, American speed skater Dan Jansen (above) posted a world record time in the men's 1000 meter race and won a gold medal in his final Olympic event ... Switzerland's Vreni Schneider won gold, silver, and bronze in women's alpine skiing ... Ekaterina Gordeeva and Sergei Grinkov, gold medalists in the 1988 Games, finished on top once again in the pairs figure skating final. The men's gold went to Alexei Urmanov. All three represented Russia ... As a result of rules reforms set in motion in the 1980s, former ice dancing gold medalists from 1984, Jayne Torvill and Christopher Dean, were eligible to compete in these Olympics, even though they had turned pro. They were both in their late thirties – a considerable handicap considering the ages of the skaters their were competing against – but they took the bronze medal ... Russia stood alone as a nation, having completed its transition out of the "Unified Team" years. (That meant, for instance, that Ukraine fielded an independent team for the first time.) The Russians led the way in total medals and gold medals.

1996: Terror.

Tragedy struck the Olympics when Christian extremist Eric Robert Rudolph extended his string of political bombings (in protest of abortion, "global socialism" and the "homosexual agenda") to Centennial Park during the 1996 Atlanta Games.

The bomb he set off killed a bystander, Alice Hawthorne. A member of the media, TV cameraman Meli Uzonyol, suffered a heart attack and died shortly after the attack. The IOC chose to continue the Atlanta Games.

The world mourned, and the Olympic flame burned, as the Games went on.

1996: Georgia On Our Mind

I DREAMT I WAS *DROWNING ... DROWNING IN A SEA* OF *UNANSWERED QUESTIONS ....*

Once-obscure Irish swimmer **Michelle Smith** took home three gold medals from the Atlanta Olympics, but she's been awfully quiet about them in recent years. Maybe she's just modest and unassuming. Then again, her reticence to talk to interviewers about the Atlanta medals may have had something to do with a little problem she had with the International Swimming Federation. A urine test she provided to officials two years after winning her medals turned out to have been doctored with alcohol. She was banned for four years from competitive swimming for tampering with the test, and although she was never stripped of her medals, her career basically ground to a standstill. Could performance-enhancing drugs have been an issue? We'll leave that to the experts. Smith's problems – and the unresolved questions connected to her status as an Olympic champion – reflect those of many past Olympians of her era.

The decision to hold the 1996 Olympics in Atlanta was a controversial one, as many observers had expected the IOC to select Athens, Greece in commemoration of the first modern Olympic games held there in 1896. (Athens would end up hosting the 2000 Summer Olympics.)

Ka-ching, revisited.

WELCOME TO THE *OLYMPICS!* HAVE A *COKE!*

Just as in Los Angeles in 1984, critics complained that these Olympic Games were dominated by the spirit of American capitalism.

124

Breakthroughs in Georgia

The Olympics looked more diverse than ever in Atlanta in 1996:

PALESTINE FIELDED AN OLYMPIC TEAM FOR THE FIRST TIME.

BOXER **MUHAMMAD ALI**, WHO HAD WON GOLD FOR THE U.S. IN 1960 IN ROME, LIT THE OLYMPIC FLAME. HE WAS THE FIRST MUSLIM TO WIN THIS HIGH OLYMPIC HONOR.

THEY CALL ME **THE POCKET HERCULES!**

FOUR-FOOT, ELEVEN INCH (150 CM) **NAIM SULEYMANOGLU** OF BULGARIA BECAME THE FIRST WEIGHTLIFTER TO WIN THREE STRAIGHT GOLD MEDALS IN HIS WEIGHT CLASS.

Golden moments....

Lilia Podkopayeya of the Ukraine took the women's all-around gymnastics gold ... The U.S. women's team took gymnastic gold in dramatic fashion ... Pro legend Andre Agassi won the gold in the men's tennis singles ... U.S. runner Michael Johnson set a world record in the men's 200 meter race, and came away from Atlanta with two gold medals ... Canada's Donovan Bailey took the gold in the men's 100 meter with a world record time ... Thirty-five-year old Carl Lewis, one of the heroes of the 1984 games, takes a gold medal in the long jump ... Amy Van Dyken won four gold medals in swimming ... China's Deng Yaping took gold medals in both the singles and doubles table tennis competition for women ... Lee Lai Shan won the sailing gold medal for Hong Kong ... Athletes from 79 of the 197 participating nations win medals ... The United States easily outpaced Russia and Germany in the gold medal count and overall medal count.

125

1998: Redemption in Japan

Did you ever see that Bill Murray film *Groundhog Day*, in which a TV reporter has to relive the same day of his life over and over again – until he gets it right? That may have been how Japanese ski-jumper Masahiko "Happy" Harada felt as he pondered his final jump of the 1998 Nagano games.

Back in 1994, the Japanese squad had seemed poised for gold when anchor jumper Harada, who had previously posted a stellar jump of 122 meters, prepared to launch. All the Japanese needed to clinch the gold was a jump of 105 meters from Harada. Apparently, it was not "Happy's" day for happiness, as he managed only a subpar jump of 98 meters that cost his team the gold medal.

Fast forward four years, to Nagano. Now representing the host nation, Harada took his first jump of the competition – and promptly disintegrated. Okay, he didn't *literally* disintegrate, but it's a good bet that some Japanese were wishing that he had. He posted a truly disastrous 79.5 meter jump, and the Japanese team sank from first place to fourth. Déjà vu all over again, right?

The millions of terrified Japanese fans who recoiled in horror at Harada's first jump of the 1998 Olympics apparently didn't see the end of the Bill Murray film: the TV reporter eventually *does* get it right. On his final jump of the Games, Harada nailed a 137-meter jump that tied an Olympic record, put Japan back in the hunt for gold, and spared the great jumper a lifetime of abuse from drunks in Japanese bars. Japan took its first ski-jumping gold since 1972.

WHAT *JINX?*

Enter the eco-Olympics: the uniforms of Nagano personnel consisted of 100% recyclable fabrics. Environmental responsibility emerges as an increasingly important organizing principle of future Olympic events.

What? No dream team?

NOPE. I'M PLAYING FOR *MY* HOME TEAM.

NHL players were allowed to compete for the first time in the men's hockey events ... but no single competing nation benefited disproportionately from the decision, as the pro athletes represented a variety of countries.

What Goes Around Comes Around

Everything old was new again in the 1998 Nagano Olympics:

TO EVERYTHING THERE
IS A SEASON ...

AFTER YEARS OF LOBBYING,
WOMEN'S *ICE HOCKEY* MADE
ITS OFFICIAL DEBUT AS AN
OLYMPIC SPORT

NORWAY'S *BJORN DAEHLIE*
CONCLUDED A STELLAR OLYMPIC
CROSS-COUNTRY SKIING CAREER WITH
12 TOTAL MEDALS, EIGHT OF WHICH
WERE GOLD.

DENMARK FINALLY WON A
MEDAL IN THE WINTER
OLYMPICS, SECURING THE
SILVER IN CURLING.

Golden moments....

American figure skater Tara Lipinski takes the ladies' finals, winning an Olympic gold medal at just fifteen years of age ... Ilia Kulik of Russia won the men's gold in figure skating; his teammates Oksana Kazakpve and Artur Dmitriev won the pairs contest ... Austria's Hermann Meier bounded back after a fall a downhill skiing run to win two gold medals ... The Czech Republic wins the men's ice hockey competition, while the United States takes the women's gold ... Snowboarding debuted as an Olympic sport; Canadian Ross Rebagliati was allowed to keep the gold medal he had won, despite having been disqualified earlier for a blood test that showed marijuana in his bloodstream ... Speed skaters from the Netherlands won five of the ten possible gold medals ... Germany edged out Norway for the lead in total gold medals and overall medals.

2000: Freeman's Finest Hour

Talk about pressure. Australian track star Cathy Freeman, who had won the silver medal in the 400-meter event in the 1996 Games at Atlanta, found herself, four years later, at the center of a genuine, full-force, Down Under media hurricane. Everywhere you went, Aussies were asking themselves: Was Freeman really host nation Australia's best chance at winning a gold medal in 2000? (Probably.) Did she really have the "world at her feet and the soul of a nation on her back," as one pundit put it? (Uh … maybe.) How would Freeman respond to all the attention? (Stay tuned!)

The answer to that last query was, fortunately for Freeman, "Remarkably well." Freeman, who was chosen to light the Olympic flame during the opening ceremonies, became the first – and, so far, the only – athlete to assume that honor and then go on to win a gold medal in the same Games. She beat Lorraine Graham of Jamaica by a little less than half a second in the 400 meters.

> OKAY, OKAY … I **WON** THE GOLD. YOU CAN ALL **RELAX**.

199 nations competed at the 2000 Sydney Games, a new high. Afghanistan's restriction on sporting events made that nation the only member country of the IOC not in attendance.

Lighting the skies...

> WOW!

Spectacular fireworks were a highlight of the eye-popping closing ceremonies in Sydney. The world-famous Sydney Opera house is visible to the left of the Olympic stadium.

David and Goliath

US WRESTLER *RULON GARDNER* CAME OUT OF NOWHERE TO DETHRONE ALEXANDER KARELIN, WHO HAD NOT LOST A MATCH IN THIRTEEN YEARS.

SWIMMER ERIC MOUSSAMBANI OF *EQUATORIAL GUINEA* SHOWED LITTLE POTENTIAL FOR A MEDAL, BUT *PLENTY OF HEART*, AS HE FINISHED THE 100 METER RACE IN AN UNDERWHELMING 112.7 SECONDS – MORE THAN TWICE THE TIME OF THE GOLD MEDAL WINNER.

CAMEROON DEFEATED MIGHTY SPAIN IN THE SOCCER (FOOTBALL) SOCCER FINAL.

Golden moments....

Swimmer Eric Moussambani of Equatorial Guinea showed little potential for a medal, but plenty of heart, as he finished the 100 meter race in an underwhelming 112.7 seconds – more than twice the time required for gold medal winner Pieter van den Hoogenband to complete the course. Australian swimmer Ian Thorpe American captured four medals, three of them gold, and shattered his own world record in the 400-meter freestyle ... Russian gymnast Alexei Nemov won six medals, equaling his take in Atlanta four years previously ... American runner Michael Johnson defended his 1996 gold medal in the 400 meters ... Marion Jones of the United States dominated with five total medals, three of them gold, and emerged as one of the heroes of the U.S. team. She will, however, be stripped of her Olympic honors when she is proven in 2007 to have taken illegal performance-enhancing drugs. Jones becomes a symbol, not of athletic excellence, but of rampant self-destruction in the pursuit of undeserved Olympic gold ... The United States won 38 gold medals and 94 medals overall to lead the field.

129

A not-so-golden moment

WE *REALLY* WANT THE OLYMPICS.

Salt Lake City (above) was named the host city of the 2002 Olympics in 1992. The American city overcame strong bids from competing cities in Switzerland, Sweden, and Canada.

In 1998, an IOC member from Switzerland announced that IOC officials had taken bribes from Salt Lake City officials in order to persuade them to select their location..

The IOC and the U.S. Justice Department announced investigations. Two top officials of the Salt Lake Organizing Committee quickly resigned.

BAD NEWS OUT OF UTAH...

TEN IOC MEMBERS WERE EVENTUALY *EXPELLED.*

TEN MORE WERE *SANCTIONED.*

NO CRIMINAL CONVICTIONS RESULTED FROM THE SCANDAL, BUT A SENSE OF A MORAL LAPSE LED TO NEW INTERNAL RULES.

Businessman Mitt Romney took over management of the debt-ridden, scandal-ridden Salt Lake City Games ... and did, by all accounts, a phenomenal job, turning a budget deficit of over $300 million into a $100 million profit.

He later launched a high-profile political career.

OFFICIALS IN NAGANO, JAPAN, EVENTUALLY ACKNOWLEDGED THAT THEY HAD SPENT OVER *$4 MILLION* TO ENTERTAIN IOC OFFICIALS IN THE EARLY 1990S.

2002: Judgment Day

"My heart breaks," television commentator and former Olympian Sandra Bezic anounced "and I'm embarrassed for our sport right now." Bezic, and most of the rest of the organized skating world, were outraged at the decision of Olympic judges to award (comparatively) low marks to the free-skate program of Canadian pair **Jamie Sale** and **David Pelletier**. The controversial marks ensured that Russians Yelena Berezhnaya and Anton Sikharulidze would win the gold medal – despite an obvious technical problem on double axel jump, an error that stood in stark contrast to the flub-free program from Sale and Pellitier, whose performance some considered to be one of the greatest in Olympic history. A major scoring scandal ensued, and ugly allegations of judge-fixing resulted in the suspension of a French judge. Sale and Pellitier were upgraded to a gold medal – even though the Russian skaters, who had had no knowledge of any wrongdoing, were permitted to keep their gold,

WHAT'S WITH THE **FRENCH JUDGE?**

American organizers prominently featured a flag taken from the site of the World Trade Center attacks on their country in 2001, leading to criticism that they had inappropriately politicized the Games.

Doping mills still have customers ....

Drug scandals continued to plague the Games, as a Spanish, and a Russian, and a British athlete were stripped of medals following positive drug tests. The Briton, Alain Baxter, is eventually exonerated. He had used the wrong cold medication.

Out of Nowhere

Salt Lake City was the stage for one of the Games' biggest upsets:

SWITZERLAND'S *SIMON AMMANN*, RANKED *26TH IN THE WORLD*, WAS NOT SUPPOSED TO BE A FACTOR IN THE SKI JUMPING COMPETITION.

HE HAD *NEVER WON* A MAJOR INTERNATIONAL EVENT.

AMMANN SCORED *GOLD MEDALS* IN BOTH THE NORMAL AND GIANT HILL EVENTS!

THAT'S WHAT I CALL PERFECT *SWISS TIMING!*

Golden moments....

Croatian alpine skier Janica Kostelic came up with an inspiring upset of her own, winning gold and silver medals despite her recent knee surgery ... Canadian ice hockey fans reclaimed past glory as their Olympic team recaptured the top spot in the tournament ... American Sara Hughes took the ladies' figure-skating medal, narrowly defeating Russian Irina Slutkaya ... German speed skater Claudia Pechstein scores two first-place finishes, making this the fourth straight Olympic Games in which she has won gold ... In the biathlon, Norway's Ole Eindar Bjorndalen takes all four golds in the men's competition ... Norway takes the most total medals, tying with Germany and the United States for most gold medals.

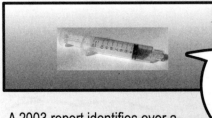

I'M NOTHING IF NOT **PERSISTENT.**

A 2003 report identifies over a hundred American athletes who failed initial drug tests, but were later cleared by internal appeals. Many of them went on to win gold medals.

It's not clear how many of the athletes named in the report had legitimate grievances with the positive results of their drug tests. Only one thing is certain ...

The doping problem continues to make headlines, destroy lives and careers, and cast long shadows over the entire Olympic movement.

THE IOC FIRES BACK:

"PEOPLE HAVE ALWAYS ATTEMPTED TO ARTIFICIALLY IMPROVE THEIR (OLYMPIC) PERFORMANCES USING RELATIVELY SIMPLE METHODS ..."

"THE HISTORY OF THE GAMES IS LITTERED WITH DOPING CASES THAT HAVE ALWAYS DAMAGED THE SPIRIT OF SPORT AS MUCH AS THE ATHLETES THEMSELVES.

"THAT IS WHY, FOR MORE THAN 30 YEARS, THE IOC HAS BEEN RADICALLY AGAINST DOPING FOR THE FOLLOWING PRINCIPLES: PROTECTING **ATHLETES' HEALTH;** RESPECTING MEDICAL AND SPORTING **ETHICS;** MAINTAINING **EQUAL OPPORTUNITIES** FOR ALL DURING COMPETITIONS."

HOW ABOUT REVOKING ALL MEDALS KNOWN TO BE TAINTED, THOUGH?

2004: Get Back ... to Athens

American swimmer Michael **Phelps** became one of the big stories of the Athens Games by winning a record-tying eight medals – six of them gold. He also tied for the highest number of individual medals – four – and set off comparisons with some of the greatest Olympic swimmers of all time, including Olympian Alexander Dityatin of Russia (Moscow, 1980) and Mark Spitz (Munich, 1972). Phelps set a world record in his 400 meter individual medley Olympic race.

The 200 meter freestyle final – which featured a thrilling battle between Phelps, Pieter van den Hoogenband of the Netherlands, and Ian Thorpe of Australia – was the subject of a great deal of attention at Athens. Thorpe took the gold, van den Hoogenband the silver, and Phelps the bronze. A little over six-tenths of a second separated the three.

I'M LOOKING FOR MORE GOLD ... IN *BEIJING.*

File under "coming full circle:" Panathanaic Stadium, where the archery competition takes place, was also the historic site of the 1896 Athens Games. The stadium is located on the very spot that, according to tradition, served as the finishing point of the original marathon ... the one that was run back in 490 B.C., after the Athenians triumphed over the Persians.

Now *that's* a dream team.

HEY -- *TIMES CHANGE.*

Argentina takes the gold medal in the basketball competition. They are the first non-U.S. squad to win the tournament since the NBA started stocking the American team with its players in 1992.

Breathtaking Finish

The race before the Games began was a spectacle in itself:

JUST **TWO MONTHS** BEFORE THE GAMES WERE TO BEGIN, MAJOR CONSTRUCTION AND PREPARATION INITIATIVES IN ATHENS WERE **STILL INCOMPLETE,** LEADING TO WORLDWIDE CONCERNS.

IN THE **RACE TO THE FINISH,** THERE WERE A COUPLE OF MINOR CONCESSIONS TO THE CALENDAR ... NOTABLY THE CHOICE TO ABANDON PLANS FOR AN (OPTIONAL) RETRACTABLE ROOF ON THE MAIN STADIUM.

IN THE END, THE GREEKS **DELIVERED AS PROMISED ...** AND ENDED UP WINNING WHAT HAD TO BE ONE OF THE MOST THRILLING, HIGH-STAKES BATTLES WITH THE CLOCK IN OLYMPIC HISTORY.

Golden moments....

U.S. swimmer Jenny Thompson capped a brilliant career by winning her twelfth gold medal; this one came by means of a team victory in the 4 x 100 meter relay ... The Iraqi soccer (football) team managed to make it to the semifinals -- quite an accomplishment, considering that their country had recently been invaded and had entered a period of prolonged carnage and turmoil ... A total of 24 athletes failed drug tests, providing a sad point of commonality with previous Games ... Justin Gatlin of the U.S. won an astonishingly close 100 meter race in which three runners finished below the ten-second mark ...

2006: China Soars

WHAT GOES UP ... COMES DOWN IN *FIRST PLACE.*

Chinese freestyle skier Han Xiaopeng spun through the air, twisted artfully and unfathomably, and stuck a solid landing. Then he did it again. At the end of his second effort in the dazzling precision-meets-acrobatics event that is freestyle skiing, Xiaopeng had edged Dmitri Dashinki of Belarus – and secured China's first skiing medal in the Winter Olympics. General chaos ensued, with the members of the freestyle team flinging their coach heavenward in celebration. (Yes, they caught him on his way down.) Xiaopeng, who had executed two flawless rounds, seemed as surprised as the rest of the onlookers at his event. "I never thought this would happen," the exuberant 22-year old told CNN. "I'm so happy to win the first gold medal for the Chinese team in history on the snow." China took eleven medals overall.

Giving hope to aging human beings of every nationality, Norway's HIlde Pedersen wins a bronze medal in cross country skiing. She is an astonishing 41 years old. Middle-aged couch potatoes around the world cheer her from their comfortable sofas ... and reach for the cheese puffs.

The flying what?

IT WAS THAT OR THE *RAPID RUTABAGA* ...

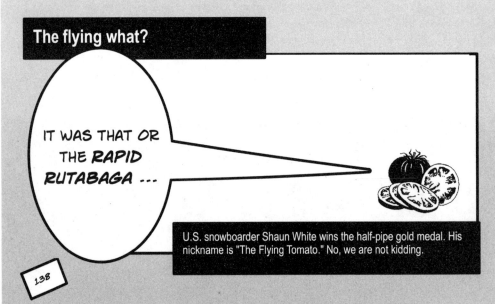

U.S. snowboarder Shaun White wins the half-pipe gold medal. His nickname is "The Flying Tomato." No, we are not kidding.

REMEMBER THOSE "LOVABLE LOSERS" OF 1988, THE **JAMAICAN BOBSLED TEAM?**

ONE MEMBER OF THAT SQUAD WAS **LASCELLE BROWN.**

BROWN EVENTUALLY APPLIED FOR CANADIAN CITIZENSHIP, TEAMED UP WITH PIERRE LUEDERS, AND **WON THE SILVER** IN THE TWO-MAN COMPETITION IN TURIN!

WHO'S LAUGHING **NOW,** MON?

Golden moments....

Evegeny Plushenko of Russia dominates the men's figure skating competition, easily winning the gold ... Snowboarder Tanja Frieden of Switzerland sneaks into first place when her chief rival, American Lindsey Jabobellis, makes a costly flub ... Duff Gibson of Canada wins the skeleton competition at 39 years of age ... Norway's Kjetl Andre Aamodt wins the Super G alpine skiing event. The victory marks his third gold in the event, and his eighth medal overall. Aamodt had first won gold fourteen years earlier, in the 1992 Winter Games ... Croatia's Janica Costelic wins another alpine gold medal, this one in the women's combined ...

What's next?

HI THERE.

The world will gather in China in 2008 for the **Beijing Olympics.**

These Games, the first ever held in China, are expected to be a showcase event for a new, globally influential China ... a nation that has overcome the adversities and controversies of the 1960s and 1970s to emerge as a global economic and cultural powerhouse. Just as the Tokyo games of 1964 helped Japan to reshape its global image after World War II, the 2008 Games will likely give the Chinese an opportunity to redefine themselves.

Beijing beat out bids from Toronto, Paris, Osaka, and Istanbul for the right to host the 2008 Games.

BEIJING'S BREATHTAKING **NATIONAL STADIUM** WILL BE THE CENTRAL VENUE OF THE GAMES.

THE SLOGAN FOR THESE OLYMPICS WILL BE *"ONE WORLD, ONE DREAM."*

AMERICAN TELEVISION NETWORK **NBC** DREW PLENTY OF ATTENTION WHEN IT PAID A STAGGERING **$5.7 BILLION** FOR THE RIGHT TO BROADCAST THE GAMES IN THE US.

THAT'S A LOT OF DRACHMAS.

Part Five:
Sport by Sport

There is no permanent list of official Olympic sports.

The roster of medal-level sports is constantly changing. Some sports, like the marathon and the long jump, have ancient pedigrees. Others, like the winter pentathlon, began as exhibition sports, but were never recognized as official medal-level events. Sports like tug-of-war and obstacle swimming were part of the early medal competitions of the modern era, but were eventually phased out.

Which sports have made the cut? And what should you know about them? Read on ...

The Summer Games

 ARCHERY IS A SPORT THAT TESTS THE ACCURACY OF COMPETITORS WHO USE A BOW TO SHOOT ARROWS. EVENTS INCLUDE: MEN'S INDIVIDUAL WOMEN'S INDIVIDUAL; MEN'S TEAM; WOMEN'S TEAM

 ATHLETICS, ALSO KNOWN AS **TRACK AND FIELD**, IS A COLLECTION OF SPORTS EVENTS THAT INVOLVE RUNNING, THROWING AND JUMPING. EVENTS INCLUDE: 100M DASH; 200M DASH; 400M DASH; 800M RUN; 1500M RUN; 5000M RUN; 10000M RUN; 100M HURDLES; 110M HURDLES; 400M HURDLES; 3000M STEEPLECHASE; HIGH JUMP; POLE VAULT; LONG JUMP; TRIPLE JUMP; SHOT PUT; DISCUS THROW; HAMMER THROW; JAVELIN THROW; HEPTATHLON (FOR WOMEN, CONSISTING OF: 100M HURDLES, HIGH JUMP, SHOT PUT, 200M RUN, LONG JUMP, JAVELIN THROW, 800M RUN); DECATHLON (FOR MEN, CONSISTING OF: 100M RUN, LONG JUMP, SHOT PUT, HIGH JUMP, 400M RUN, 110 M HURDLES, DISCUS THROW, POLE VAULT, JAVELIN THROW, 1500M RUN); 20KM RACE WALK; 50KM RACE WALK; MARATHON.

 BADMINTON IS A RACQUET SPORT USING A SHUTTLECOCK; PLAYERS TAKE POSITIONS ON OPPOSITE HALVES OF A RECTANGULAR COURT DIVIDED BY A NET. EVENTS INCLUDE: MEN'S SINGLES; MEN'S DOUBLES; WOMEN'S SINGLES; WOMEN'S DOUBLES; MIXED DOUBLES.

BASEBALL IS A BAT-AND-BALL SPORT PLAYED BETWEEN TWO TEAMS OF NINE PLAYERS EACH. IN THE OLYMPICS, THIS SPORT IS OPEN TO MEN. WOMEN DO NOT COMPETE IN THE BASEBALL TOURNAMENT, BUT RATHER IN SOFTBALL.

BOXING IS A REGULATED COMBAT SPORT IN WHICH TWO PARTICIPANTS (GENERALLY) OF SIMILAR WEIGHT FIGHT EACH OTHER WITH THEIR FISTS. AT PRESENT IT IS A MEN'S SPORT IN THE OLYMPICS. EVENTS INCLUDE: LIGHT FLYWEIGHT; FLYWEIGHT; BANTAMWEIGHT; FEATHERWEIGHT; LIGHTWEIGHT; LIGHT WELTERWEIGHT; WELTERWEIGHT; MIDDLEWEIGHT; LIGHT HEAVYWEIGHT; HEAVYWEIGHT.

 CANOEING/ KAYAKING IS A SPORT IN WHICH PARTICIPANTS USE A PADDLE TO PROPEL A SMALL WATERCRAFT. EVENTS INCLUDE: SLALOM AND FLATWATER CONTESTS AT VARIOUS DISTANCES FOR BOTH MEN AND WOMEN.

CYCLING IS A RACING AND RIDING SPORT USING BICYCLES. OLYMPIC CYCLING EVENTS TAKE THE FORM OF TRACK, ROAD, AND MOUNTAIN BIKE COMPETITIONS, AND ARE OPEN TO MEN AND WOMEN, WHO COMPETE SEPARATELY.

DIVING IS THE SPORT OF PERFORMING ACROBATICS WHILE JUMPING OR FALLING INTO WATER FROM A PLATFORM OR SPRINGBOARD OF A CERTAIN HEIGHT. EVENTS INCLUDE: 3M SYNCHRONIZED SPRINGBOARD; 10M SYNCHRONIZED PLATFORM; 3M SPRINGBOARD; 10M PLATFORM. MEN AND WOMEN COMPETE SEPARATELY IN THESE EVENTS.

EQUESTRIANISM IS A SPORT BASED ON HORSE-RIDING SKILLS. EVENTS INCLUDE: DRESSAGE; JUMPING; EVENTING. MEN AND WOMEN COMPETE DIRECTLY AGAINST EACH OTHER.

FENCING IS A SPORT BASED ON EUROPEAN SCHOOLS OF SWORDSMANSHIP. EVENTS INCLUDE: MEN'S EPEE; MEN'S FOIL; MEN'S SABRE; WOMEN'S EPEE; WOMEN'S FOIL; WOMEN'S SABRE. THERE ARE ALSO TEAM COMPETITIONS WITHIN EACH OF THESE DISCIPLINES.

FIELD HOCKEY IS AN OPEN-FIELD SPORT USING CURVED STICKS AND A BALL THAT WAS ORIGINALLY DEVELOPED IN ENGLISH PUBLIC SCHOOLS IN THE NINETEENTH CENTURY. TEAMS TRY TO SCORE POINTS BY PLACING THE BALL IN AN OPPONENT'S GOAL. EVENTS INCLUDE: MEN'S TOURNAMENT; WOMEN'S TOURNAMENT.

GYMNASTICS IS A SPORT IN WHICH COMPETITORS PERFORM SPECIALIZED PHYSICAL ROUTINES BEFORE JUDGES. VARIATIONS ON TRADITIONAL "ARTISTIC" GYMNASTICS INCLUDE RHYTHMIC GYMNASTICS AND TRAMPOLINE. "ARTISTIC" EVENTS INCLUDE: MEN'S TEAM ALL-AROUND; MEN'S INDIVIDUAL ALL-AROUND; MEN'S FLOOR ROUTINE; MEN'S RINGS; MEN'S VAULT; MEN'S PARALLEL BARS; MEN'S HORIZONTAL BARS; WOMEN'S TEAM ALL-AROUND; WOMEN'S INDIVIDUAL ALL-AROUND; WOMEN'S VAULT; WOMEN'S UNEVEN BARS; WOMEN'S BALANCE BEAM; WOMEN'S FLOOR ROUTINE.

HANDBALL IS A TEAM SPORT WHERE TWO TEAMS OF SEVEN PLAYERS EACH (SIX PLAYERS AND A GOALKEEPER) PASS AND BOUNCE A BALL, TRYING TO THROW IT IN THE GOAL OF THE OPPOSING TEAM. EVENTS INCLUDE: MEN'S TOURNAMENT; WOMEN'S TOURNAMENT.

JUDO IS A COMPETITIVE MARTIAL ART THAT ORIGINATED IN JAPAN IN THE LATE NINETEENTH CENTURY. EVENTS INCLUDE: MEN'S AND WOMEN'S INDIVIDUAL TOURNAMENTS, EACH WITHIN PREDETERMINED WEIGHT CLASSES

THE **MODERN PENTATHLON** IS A SPORTS CONTEST CONSISTING OF FIVE EVENTS: FENCING, PISTOL SHOOTING, SWIMMING, SHOW HORSE JUMPING, AND A CROSS-COUNTRY FOOTRACE. NONE OF THE EVENTS OF THE MODERN PENTATHLON WERE PART OF THE ANCIENT OLYMPICS. EVENTS INCLUDE: MEN'S PENTATHLON, WOMEN'S PENTATHLON.

ROWING IS A SPORT IN WHICH ATHLETES RACE AGAINST EACH OTHER ON BODIES OF WATER, PROPELLING THEIR BOAT WITH OARS. THERE ARE A VARIETY OF EVENTS; MEN AND WOMEN COMPETE SEPARATELY.

SAILBOAT RACING IS A BOAT-RACING SPORT IN WHICH THE VESSELS OF COMPETITORS ARE PROPELLED BY THE WIND. VARIOUS EVENTS ARE PART OF THE COMPETITION, INCLUDING MEN'S RACING EVENTS, WOMEN'S RACING EVENTS, AND OPEN EVENTS.

SHOOTING IS A SPORT THAT TESTS ACCURACY AND SPEED WITH FIREARMS AND AIR RIFLES. VARIOUS MEN'S AND WOMEN'S SHOOTING EVENTS ARE PART OF THE OLYMPIC COMPETITION.

 SOCCER, KNOWN OUTSIDE OF THE UNITED STATES AS FOOTBALL, IS A TEAM SPORT PLAYED WITH A BALL. IT INVOLVES TWO TEAMS OF ELEVEN PLAYERS. PLAYERS ATTEMPT TO SCORE GOALS BY KICKING OR "HEADING" THE BALL. EVENTS INCLUDE: MEN'S TOURNAMENT; WOMEN'S TOURNAMENT.

 SOFTBALL IS A TEAM SPORT SIMILAR TO BASEBALL USING A LARGER, SLIGHTLY SOFTER BALL. THE SOFTBALL TOURNAMENT IS OPEN ONLY TO WOMEN IN THE OLYMPICS; MEN COMPETE IN THE BASEBALL TOURNAMENT.

 SWIMMING IS AN INDIVIDUAL AQUATIC RACING SPORT. EVENTS INCLUDE: FREESTYLE (50 M, 100 M, 200 M, 400 M, 800 M [WOMEN ONLY], 1500 M [MEN ONLY], 4X100 M RELAY, 4X200 M RELAY, 10 KM MARATHON; BACKSTROKE (100 M, 200 M); BREASTSTROKE (100 M, 200 M); BUTTERFLY (100 M, 200 M); MEDLEY (200 M INDIVIDUAL, 400 M INDIVIDUAL, 4 X 100 M RELAY).

SYNCHRONIZED SWIMMING IS A HYBRID OF SWIMMING, GYMNASTICS, AND DANCE THAT IS CURRENTLY ONLY OPEN TO MALE COMPETITORS. EVENTS INCLUDE: WOMEN'S TEAM; WOMEN'S DUET.

 TABLE TENNIS (ALSO KNOWN AS PING-PONG) IS A SPORT IN WHICH TWO OR FOUR PLAYERS HIT A LIGHTWEIGHT, HOLLOW BALL BACK AND FORTH TO EACH OTHER WITH PADDLES OR RACKETS. EVENTS INCLUDE: MEN'S SINGLES; MEN'S TEAMS; WOMEN'S SINGLES; WOMEN'S TEAMS.

 TAEKWANDO IS A KOREAN MARTIAL ART AND COMBAT SPORT. EVENTS INCLUDE: MEN'S AND WOMEN'S INDIVIDUAL TOURNAMENTS, EACH WITHIN PREDETERMINED WEIGHT CLASSES.

 TENNIS IS A GAME PLAYED BETWEEN TWO PLAYERS (SINGLES) OR BETWEEN TWO TEAMS OF TWO PLAYERS (DOUBLES). PLAYERS USE A STRUNG RACQUET TO STRIKE A HOLLOW RUBBER BALL COVERED WITH FELT OVER A NET INTO THE OPPONENT'S COURT. EVENTS INCLUDE: MEN'S SINGLES; MEN'S DOUBLES; WOMEN'S SINGLES; WOMEN'S DOUBLES . THERE IS CURRENTLY NO MIXED DOUBLES COMPETITION IN THE OLYMPICS.

A **TRIATHLON** IS AN ENDURANCE SPORTS EVENT CONSISTING OF SWIMMING, CYCLING AND RUNNING OVER VARIOUS DISTANCES. THERE ARE SEPARATE MEN'S AND WOMEN'S TRIATHLON EVENTS IN THE OLYMPICS.

VOLLEYBALL IS A TEAM SPORT IN WHICH TWO TEAMS OF SIX ACTIVE PLAYERS, SEPARATED BY A HIGH NET, EACH TRY TO SCORE POINTS AGAINST ONE ANOTHER BY GROUNDING A BALL ON THE OTHER TEAM'S COURT UNDER ORGANIZED RULES. THERE ARE INDOOR VOLLEYBALL AND BEACH VOLLEYBALL TOURNAMENTS AT THE OLYMPICS, EACH INCORPORATING MEN'S AND WOMEN'S TEAMS.

WATER POLO IS A TEAM WATER SPORT IN WHICH TEAMS TRY TO SCORE GOALS WITH A BALL; PLAY OCCURS IN A SWIMMING POOL. THERE ARE MEN'S AND WOMEN'S WATER POLO TOURNAMENTS IN THE OLYMPICS.

WEIGHTLIFTING IS A SPORT IN WHICH COMPETITORS ATTEMPT TO LIFT HEAVY WEIGHTS MOUNTED ON STEEL BARS CALLED BARBELLS. EVENTS INCLUDE: MEN'S AND WOMEN'S INDIVIDUAL TOURNAMENTS, EACH WITHIN PREDETERMINED WEIGHT CLASSES.

WRESTLING AT THE OLYMPICS TAKES TWO FORMS: GRECO-ROMAN AND FREESTYLE. THE GRECO-ROMAN STYLE FORBIDS ATTACKS BELOW THE WAIST, AND RELIES MORE HEAVILY ON THROWS. MEN COMPETE IN BOTH FREESTYLE AND GRECO-ROMAN TOURNAMENTS AT THE OLYMPICS. WOMEN COMPETE ONLY IN FREESTYLE.

NEW SUMMER OLYMPIC SPORTS

ARE ALWAYS UNDER CONSIDERATION BY THE IOC. THE SPORTS LISTED HERE ARE THE ONES THAT HAVE BEEN APPROVED AS ACTIVE, OFFICIAL, MEDAL-LEVEL SPORTS *AS OF PRESS TIME FOR THIS BOOK.*

The Winter Games

ALPINE SKIING OR **DOWNHILL SKIING** IS A SPORT IN WHICH COMPETITORS SLIDE DOWN SNOW-COVERED HILLS ON LONG SKIS. EVENTS INCLUDE GIANT SLALOM RACES (WHICH INVOLVES SKIING THROUGH SETS OF WIDELY PLACED POLES); SUPER G RACES (WITH GATES AS WIDE AS IN SLALOM, BUT ON A COURSE INCORPORATING FEWER TURNS AND A LONGER COURSE); SLALOM RACES (WHICH REQUIRE SKIERS TO THREAD THEIR WAY BETWEEN NARROWLY PLACED POLES); AND DOWNHILL (WHICH REQUIRES COMPETITORS TO NAVIGATE BROADLY SPACED GATES, TIGHT TURNS, AND ICY CONDITIONS AT EXTREMELY HIGH SPEEDS, ON A COURSE THAT FEATURES JUMPS). THERE ARE MEN'S AND WOMEN'S EVENTS IN EACH OF THESE CATEGORIES.

BIATHLON IS BEST KNOWN AS A WINTER SPORT THAT COMBINES CROSS-COUNTRY SKIING AND RIFLE SHOOTING. THERE ARE MEN'S AND WOMEN'S COMPETITIONS. EVENTS INCLUDE: MILITARY PATROL; MEN'S INDIVIDUAL; MEN'S RELAY; MEN'S SPRINT; MEN'S PURSUIT; MEN'S MASS START; WOMEN'S INDIVIDUAL; WOMEN'S RELAY; WOMEN'S SPRINT; WOMEN'S PURSUIT; WOMEN'S MASS START.

BOBSLED OR **BOBSLEIGH** IS A SPORT IN WHICH TEAMS MAKE TIMED RUNS DOWN NARROW, TWISTING, ICED TRACKS IN A GRAVITY-POWERED SLED. AT THE WINTER OLYMPICS, THE SPORT HAS TWO-MAN, FOUR-MAN, AND TWO-WOMAN VARIATIONS.

CROSS-COUNTRY SKIING

IS A LONG-DISTANCE RACING SPORT FOR SKIERS POPULAR IN MANY COUNTRIES WITH LARGE SNOWFIELDS, PRIMARILY NORTHERN EUROPE, CANADA AND ALASKA. IN THE OLYMPICS, MEN AND WOMEN COMPETE SEPARATELY, AT VARIOUS DISTANCES, IN INDIVIDUAL AND TEAM EVENTS.

CURLING IS A TEAM SPORT WITH SIMILARITIES TO BOWLS AND BOCCE, PLAYED ON A RECTANGULAR SHEET OF CAREFULLY PREPARED ICE BY TWO TEAMS OF FOUR PLAYERS EACH. THE COMPLEX NATURE OF STONE PLACEMENT AND SHOT SELECTION HAS LED SOME TO REFER TO CURLING AS "CHESS ON ICE." THERE ARE SEPARATE MEN'S AND WOMEN'S OLYMPIC COMPETITIONS.

FIGURE SKATING IS A SPORT IN WHICH INDIVIDUALS OR PAIRS EXECUTE SPINS, JUMPS, FOOTWORK AND OTHER CHOREOGRAPHY ON ICE. THE SCORING, WHICH IS PERFORMED BY JUDGES, IS COMPLEX. MEN'S SINGLES, WOMEN SINGLES, AND PAIRS COMPETITIONS ARE POPULAR EVENTS. ICE DANCING IS CONSIDERED PART OF THIS SPORT, ALTHOUGH IT HAS A MUCH DIFFERENT AESTHETIC AND DIFFERENT RULES. (FOR INSTANCE, ICE DANCERS ARE NOT ALLOWED TO USE THROWS OR JUMPS.)

FREESTYLE SKIING AROSE WHEN SKIERS BEGAN COMBINING ACROBATIC MOVES WITH SKI-JUMPING TRAINING SESSIONS. LATER, NON-COMPETITIVE PROFESSIONAL SKIING EXHIBITIONS IN THE UNITED STATES FEATURED PERFORMANCES OF WHAT WOULD LATER BE CALLED FREESTYLE. THE SPORT OF FREESTYLE SKIING, IN WHICH PARTICIPANTS ARE GIVEN SCORES BY JUDGES, IS NOW THE FOCUS OF SUCH OLYMPIC EVENTS AS MEN'S MOGULS, MEN'S AERIALS, WOMEN'S MOGULS, AND WOMEN'S AERIALS.

ICE HOCKEY, OFTEN REFERRED TO SIMPLY AS HOCKEY IN CANADA AND THE UNITED STATES, IS A TEAM SPORT PLAYED ON ICE WITH A PUCK AND TWO GOALS. THE OBJECT IS TO SHOOT THE PUCK INTO THE OPPONENT'S GOAL. MEN'S AND WOMEN'S ICE HOCKEY TOURNAMENTS TAKE PLACE IN THE WINTER OLYMPICS.

LUGE IS A WINTER SPORT THAT INVOLVES RACING WHILE SLEDDING SUPINE AND FEET-FIRST. IN THE OLYMPICS, THERE ARE MEN'S SINGLES, WOMEN'S SINGLES, AND DOUBLES COMPETITIONS. TECHNICALLY, WOMEN CAN COMPETE IN DOUBLES RACES IN THE LUGE, BUT AS A PRACTICAL MATTER TWO-PERSON LUGE CONTESTS GENERALLY INVOLVE TWO MEN.

NORDIC COMBINED

SKIING IS A SPORT IN WHICH ATHLETES COMPETE IN BOTH CROSS-COUNTRY SKIING AND SKI JUMPING. AT THE OLYMPICS, THERE ARE INDIVIDUAL, TEAM, AND SPRINT EVENTS FOR MEN; WOMEN DO NOT NOW COMPETE IN THE EVENT.

SHORT TRACK SPEED

SKATING IS A FORM OF ICE-SKATE RACING THAT TAKES PLACE ON AN OVAL ICE TRACK. IN COMPETITIONS, MULTIPLE SKATERS (TYPICALLY BETWEEN FOUR AND SIX) SKATE SIMULTANEOUSLY. EVENTS INCLUDE: MEN'S 500 M; MEN'S 1000 M; MEN'S 1500 M; MEN'S 3000 M; MEN'S 5000 M RELAY; WOMEN'S 500 M; WOMEN'S 1000 M; WOMEN'S 3000 M; WOMEN'S 3000 M RELAY.

SKELETON IS A RACING SPORT IN WHICH COMPETITORS AIM TO DRIVE A ONE-PERSON SLED IN A PRONE, HEAD-FIRST POSITION DOWN AN ICE TRACK IN THE FASTEST TIME. THIS DIFFERS FROM LUGE, WHERE THE RIDER DRIVES THE SLED FROM A SUPINE, FEET-FIRST ORIENTATION. THE OLYMPICS FEATURE BOTH MEN'S AND WOMEN'S SKELETON COMPETITIONS.

SKI JUMPING IS A SPORT IN WHICH SKIERS GO DOWN AN INRUN WITH A TAKE-OFF RAMP (THE JUMP), ATTEMPTING TO GO AS FAR AS POSSIBLE WHILE WINNING MAXIMUM STYLE POINTS FROM JUDGES. CURRENTLY, IT IS ONLY CONTESTED BY MEN IN THE OLYMPICS. EVENTS INCLUDE INDIVIDUAL LARGE HILL, INDIVIDUAL NORMAL HILL, AND TEAM LARGE HILL.

SNOWBOARDING IS A SPORT IN WHICH INDIVIDUAL COMPETITORS SPEED DOWN A SNOW-COVERED SLOPE ON A SNOWBOARD THAT IS ATTACHED TO THEIR FEET. IT IS SIMILAR TO SKIING, BUT WAS INSPIRED BY SURFING AND SKATEBOARDING. EVENTS INCLUDE THE HALFPIPE; THE GIANT SLALOM; THE PARALLEL GIANT SLALOM; AND THE SNOWBOARD CROSS. MEN AND WOMEN COMPETE SEPARATELY.

SPEED SKATING, ALSO KNOWN AS **LONG-TRACK SPEED SKATING** IS A SPORT IN WHICH COMPETITORS RACE TO ACHIEVE THE FASTEST TIME WHILE SKATING OVER A SET DISTANCE. EVENTS INCLUDE: MEN'S 500 M; MEN'S 1000 M; MEN'S 1500 M; MEN'S 5000 M; MEN'S 10000 M; MEN'S TEAM PURSUIT; WOMEN'S 500 M; WOMEN'S 1000 M; WOMEN'S 1500 M; WOMEN'S 3000 M; WOMEN'S 5000 M; WOMEN'S TEAM PURSUIT.

NEW WINTER OLYMPIC SPORTS ARE LESS COMMON THAN NEW SPORTS IN THE SUMMER GAMES, BUT ARE NEVERTHELESS CONSTANTLY UNDER CONSIDERATION BY THE IOC.

Part Six: Test Your Olympic Knowledge

I'M THE UGANDAN ATHLETE WHO WAS THE FIRST TO TAKE AN OLYMPIC "VICTORY LAP." IT HAPPENED AFTER I WON AN UPSET VICTORY IN THE 1972 400-METER HURDLE FINALS IN MUNICH, SETTING A WORLD RECORD TIME. *WHO AM I?*

I WON THE WOMEN'S 100 METER GOLD FOR POLAND IN 1932. WHEN I DIED IN 1980, AN AUTOPSY REVEALED THAT I HAD A RARE GENETIC CONDITION THAT GAVE ME BOTH MALE AND FEMALE CHROMOSOMES. BY TODAY'S STANDARDS, I WOULD HAVE TO COMPETE AS A MAN. *WHO AM I?*

I WAS THE FIRST PERSON TO WIN A GOLD MEDAL FOR MY HOME COUNTRY OF ALGERIA. IT HAPPENED IN 1992 IN THE 1500 METER FINALS. **WHO AM I?**

WE LEARNED THAT WE HAD BEATEN FRANCE FOR THE **BRONZE** MEDAL IN THE 1992 WOMEN'S 4 X 400 RELAY BY FOUR-HUNDREDTHS OF A SECOND ... AND PROMPTLY WENT NUTS IN CELEBRATION ON THE FIELD. **WHAT COUNTRY ARE WE FROM?**

QUESTION FIVE.

WHO SAYS THE KIWI, THE NATIONAL SYMBOL OF NEW ZEALAND, IS FLIGHTLESS? WITHIN SIX HOURS OF EACH OTHER, WE RAN TO WIN UNLIKELY GOLD MEDALS FOR NEW ZEALAND IN 1960. **WHO ARE WE?**

QUESTION SIX.

AT THE UNHEARD-OF AGE OF 43, I LED THE ITALIAN DOWNHILL RELAY SKIING TEAM TO GOLD IN 1994. **WHO AM I?**

IN 1992, DESPITE **COMPLETE RECONSTRUCTIVE KNEE SURGERY,** I BECAME THE FIRST CANADIAN ATHLETE TO WIN GOLD IN A DOWNHILL SKIING EVENT. **WHO AM I?**

I WON THE FIRST GOLD MEDAL FOR **KAZAKHSTAN,** TAKING FIRST PLACE IN THE 50 KILOMETER CROSS-COUNTRY FINALS IN 1994. FUNNY THING WAS, I DECLARED MYSELF A RUSSIAN CITIZEN, EVEN THOUGH I WAS BORN IN KAZAKHSTAN. **WHO AM I?**

How Did You Do?

QUESTION ONE: JOHN AKII-BUA

QUESTION TWO: STANISŁAWA WALASIEWICZ (ALSO KNOWN AS STELLA WALSH)

QUESTION THREE: HASSIBA BOULMERKA

QUESTION FOUR: NIGERIA

QUESTION FIVE: MURRAY HALBERG AND PETER SNELL

QUESTION SIX: MAURILIO DE ZOLT

QUESTION SEVEN: KERRIN LEE-GARTNER

QUESTION EIGHT: VLADIMIR SMIRNOV

ZERO TO FOUR CORRECT: NO MEDAL.

FIVE TO SIX CORRECT: BRONZE.

SIX TO SEVEN CORRECT: SILVER.

ALL EIGHT CORRECT: YOU TOOK THE GOLD!

165

Bibliography and
Recommended Reading

CHECK OUT THESE GREAT BOOKS ABOUT THE OLYMPICS AT YOUR LOCAL LIBRARY!

R. MANDELL, *THE FIRST MODERN OLYMPICS* (1976)

J. LUCAS, *THE MODERN OLYMPIC GAMES* (1980)

J. J. MACALOON, *THIS GREAT SYMBOL* (1981)

A. GUTTMANN, *THE GAMES MUST GO ON* (1984)

J. FINDLING, K. PELLING, *HISTORICAL DICTIONARY OF THE MODERN OLYMPIC MOVEMENT* (1996)

D. WALLECHINSKY, *THE COMPLETE BOOK OF THE SUMMER OLYMPICS* (1996)

D. WALLECHINSKY, *THE COMPLETE BOOK OF THE WINTER OLYMPICS* (1998)

J. SWADDLING, *THE ANCIENT OLYMPIC GAMES* (2000)
A. KITROEFF, *WRESTLING WITH THE ANCIENTS: MODERN GREEK IDENTITY AND THE OLYMPICS* (2004)

S. G. MILLER, *ANCIENT GREEK ATHLETICS* (2004)

T. PERROTET, *THE NAKED OLYMPICS* (2004)

N. SPIVEY, *THE ANCIENT OLYMPICS* (2004)

INTERNATIONAL OLYMPIC COMMITTEE
WWW.OLYMPICS.ORG

WIKIPEDIA: THE OLYMPIC GAMES
EN.WIKIPEDIA.ORG/WIKI/OLYMPIC_GAMES

DICOLYMPIC
WWW.DICOLYMPIC.COM

AROUND THE RINGS: THE BUSINESS OF THE OLYMPICS
WWW.AROUNDTHERINGS.COM

DATABASE OLYMPICS
WWW.DATABASEOLYMPICS.COM

OLYMPICS MEMORIES
WWW.OLYMPICSMEMORIES.COM

BRANDON YUSUF TOROPOV

IS FOUNDER AND CEO OF IWORDSMITH.COM, A
CONTENT CREATION AND BOOK DEVELOPMENT FIRM.
HE IS THE AUTHOR OF OVER A DOZEN PUBLISHED
BOOKS, INCLUDING "SHAKESPEARE FOR BEGINNERS,"
"THE COMPLETE IDIOT'S GUIDE TO WORLD RELIGIONS,"
AND "THE COMPLETE IDIOT'S GUIDE TO THE KORAN." HE
LIVES IN MASSACHUSETTS. E-MAIL HIM AT
BTOROPOV@IWORDSMITH.COM - AND LET HIM KNOW
WHAT YOU THOUGHT OF THIS BOOK.

JOE LEE IS AN ILLUSTRATOR AND AUTHOR

WITH MANY YEARS OF EXPERIENCE. HE IS THE AUTHOR
OF "THE HISTORY OF CLOWNS FOR BEGINNERS" (A
SUBJECT HE KNOWS WELL AS A GRADUATE OF
RINGLING BROS., BARNUM AND BAILEY CLOWN
COLLEGE AND A VETERAN OF RINGLING, KING BROS.-
COLE, AND HOXIE BROS. CIRCUSES) AND "DANTE FOR
BEGINNERS." HE IS ALSO THE ILLUSTRATOR OF
SEVEN OTHER TITLES IN THE ONGOING SERIES
PUBLISHED BY FOR BEGINNERS LLC INCLUDING THE
RECENTLY RELEASED "DADA AND SURREALISM FOR
BEGINNERS" AND "SHAKESPEARE FOR BEGINNERS."
JOE IS THE EDITORIAL CARTOONIST FOR THE
BLOOMINGTON HERALD-TIMES (WINNING THE "BEST
CARTOON OF THE YEAR" FROM THE INDIANA BRANCH
OF THE SOCIETY OF PROFESSIONAL JOURNALISTS FOR
2006) AND THE STAFF ILLUSTRATOR FOR OUR
BROWNCOUNTY MAGAZINE AND INTO ART. HE HAS
WORKED FOR PUBLICATIONS AS VARIED AS THE PHI
DELTA KAPPAN, SKEPTIC, CRICKET, AND TECHNOS. JOE
LIVES IN BLOOMINGTON, INDIANA WITH HIS WIFE
BESS, SON BRANDON, CAT GEORGE, AND THE
TERRIBLE TERRIERS, JACK AND MAX.